Lecture Notes in Computer Science 16390

The series Lecture Notes in Computer Science (LNCS), including its subseries Lecture Notes in Artificial Intelligence (LNAI) and Lecture Notes in Bioinformatics (LNBI), has established itself as a medium for the publication of new developments in computer science and information technology research, teaching, and education.

LNCS enjoys close cooperation with the computer science R & D community, the series counts many renowned academics among its volume editors and paper authors, and collaborates with prestigious societies. Its mission is to serve this international community by providing an invaluable service, mainly focused on the publication of conference and workshop proceedings and postproceedings. LNCS commenced publication in 1973.

Kamal Nasrollahi · Lars Mathiassen ·
Jens Nygren
Editors

Responsible AI for Value Creation

First Interdisciplinary Workshop, REPAI-W 2025
Copenhagen, Denmark, December 1, 2025
Proceedings

Springer

Editors
Kamal Nasrollahi
Aalborg University
Aalborg, Denmark

Lars Mathiassen
Georgia State University
Atlanta, GA, USA

Jens Nygren
Halmstad University
Halmstad, Sweden

ISSN 0302-9743 ISSN 1611-3349 (electronic)
Lecture Notes in Computer Science
ISBN 978-3-032-16885-6 ISBN 978-3-032-16886-3 (eBook)
https://doi.org/10.1007/978-3-032-16886-3

This Springer imprint is published by the registered company Springer Nature Switzerland AG
The registered company address is: Gewerbestrasse 11, 6330 Cham, Switzerland

Preface

The accelerating impact of AI has made responsible technology an inherently interdisciplinary challenge. Developing AI systems is no longer solely a technical endeavor; meaningful and trustworthy AI requires the integration of legal requirements, ethical principles, organizational realities, and societal value considerations from the outset. However, research that genuinely spans disciplinary boundaries often struggles to find an appropriate publication venue, particularly when it does not fit neatly within a single academic field. The First Interdisciplinary Workshop on Responsible AI for Value Creation (REPAI-W) addressed this gap by offering a dedicated forum for research that bridges these perspectives. It encouraged contributions that advance AI solutions while engaging with at least two complementary disciplines—such as technical AI development, ethics, law, organizational studies, and value creation—to deepen the understanding of AI's role in real-world practice and shape its responsible use.

REPAI-W was held in Copenhagen, Denmark, on December 1st, 2025, as a standalone workshop. In its first edition, the workshop received nine valid submissions, of which six were accepted for presentation and publication through a rigorous double-blind review process. Each paper was evaluated by at least two reviewers, with some receiving up to four reviews. The accepted papers were presented during the workshop hosted by Aalborg University in Copenhagen. Each presentation was allocated a 30-minute slot, comprising 20 minutes for the talk and 10 minutes for discussion. The program also featured one invited talk and invited paper included in the proceedings. A total of 50 participants attended the workshop.

We would like to express our sincere gratitude to all authors who submitted their work to REPAI-W, to all reviewers for their valuable assessments, and to Aalborg University for hosting the event.

December 2025

Kamal Nasrollahi
Lars Mathiassen
Jens Nygren

Preface

Organization

Chairs

Kamal Nasrollahi	Aalborg University, Milestone Systems A/S, Denmark
Lars Mathiassen	Georgia State University, USA
Jens Nygren	Halmstad University, Sweden

Steering Committee

Thomas B. Moeslund	Aalborg University, Denmark
Jeppe Agger Nielsen	Aalborg University, Denmark
Thomas Ploug	Aalborg University, Denmark

Program Committee

Albert Ali Salah	Utrecht University, The Netherlands
Andreas Specker	Fraunhofer IOSB, Germany
Andreas Aakerberg	Aalborg University, Denmark
Andreas Møgelmose	Aalborg University, Denmark
Brian Clipp	Kitware, USA
Emil Dumic	University North, Croatia
Hesham Shehata	Asilla, Japan
Ishan Rajendrakumar Dave	Adobe Inc., USA
Ivan Nikolov	Aalborg University, Denmark
Jens Nygren	Halmstad University, Sweden
Masih Aminbeidokhti	École de technologie supérieure, Canada
Moetez Kdayem	École de technologie supérieure, Canada
Neelu Madan	Aalborg University, Denmark
Praveen Tirupattur	University of Central Florida, USA
Prerana Mukherjee	Jawaharlal Nehru University, India
Radu Tudor Ionescu	University of Bucharest, Romania
Rafael Menelau Oliveira	École de technologie supérieure, Canada
Raghavendra Kulkarni	T-Mobile USA Inc., USA
Rama Chellappa	Johns Hopkins University, USA
Ramya Akula	Ohio State University, USA

Roderic Collins	Kitware Inc., USA
Ross Greer	University of California, Merced, USA
Sonain Jamil	Université Jean Monnet Saint-Étienne, France
Srikanth Muralidharan	ETS Montreal, Canada
Surojit Saha	University of Utah, USA
Thomas Dubail	École de technologie supérieure, Canada
Vasileios Mezaris	Centre for Research and Technology Hellas, Greece
Victor Sanchez	University of Warwick, UK
Weijun Tan	Linksprite Technologies, USA
Xiwen Li	University of Utah, USA
Yang Liu	Australian National University & Data61, Australia
Yuqi Ouyang	Sichuan University, China

Contents

Contents

Conceptual Misalignment in XAI

Rolf Hvidtfeldt[1](✉), Mohammad N. S. Jahromi[1], Àlex Pujol Vidal[1], Stine N. Christensen[1], Jeppe Agger Nielsen[1], Thomas Gammeltoft-Hansen[2], Thomas Ploug[1], and Thomas B. Moeslund[1]

[1] Aalborg University, Copenhagen, Denmark
{rolfh,ploug}@hum.aau.dk, {mosa,alexpv,stinenc,tbm}@create.aau.dk, agger@society.aau.dk

[2] University of Copenhagen, Copenhagen, Denmark
tgh@jur.ku.dk

Abstract. This paper argues that the prevailing XAI paradigm suffers not from technical limitations but from a profound philosophical misconception: the assumption that explanation is primarily about transparency. We argue that the development of useful explanation is not fundamentally a question of information transfer, but of epistemic parity. Through a case of harbor monitoring we show that stakeholders are indeed conceptually misaligned; however, these misalignments ultimately reflect underlying conflicts between domain-specific assumptions and authority claims. We call for replacing transparency-focused XAI with a new paradigm of Domain Authority Negotiation (DAN) that explicitly acknowledges explanation as a contestation of epistemic power rather than a mechanism of revelation.

Keywords: Interdisciplinarity · Explanation · XAI · Conceptual misalignment · Epistemic authority · Epistemic parity

1 Introduction

Interdisciplinary collaboration is inherently challenging not only because of differing vocabularies, skills, background knowledge, and assumptions, but also because it involves competing authority frameworks. Researchers are trained—and disciplined—to use terminology and theory in particular ways and to assert their domain's *epistemic authority*, i.e., the implicit power to determine what qualifies as valid knowledge and how it should be used. This often leads to (sometimes subconscious) issues of professional identity and mutual disrespect, producing persistent conceptual misalignments that undermine effective collaboration [14,15,17,44].

Consider the term "explanation". Though defined similarly across disciplines, its function and use depends on the authority it serves: technical explanations

R. Hvidtfeldt, M. N. S. Jahromi and À. Pujol Vidal—Equal contributions.

K. Nasrollahi et al. (Eds.): REPAI-W 2025, LNCS 16390, pp. 1–23, 2026.
https://doi.org/10.1007/978-3-032-16886-3_1

prioritize mathematical validity; legal ones, doctrinal reasoning; organizational ones, governance alignment; and ethical ones, value frameworks. These cannot be reconciled through technical refinement alone because they rest on incompatible authority claims. Even policy efforts such as the EU's Guidelines for Trustworthy AI [7] and the AI Act [1] frame "explanation" as a transparency issue rather than a question of epistemic balance, reinforcing the illusion that better algorithms can satisfy all stakeholders. Despite numerous techniques and metrics promising explainability, most fail to deliver genuine accountability or understanding. Heatmaps, saliency scores, and attribution graphs offer a veneer of interpretability—legible to developers but largely irrelevant, sometimes even misleading, to end-users, regulators, and other stakeholders.

This paper argues that prevailing XAI paradigms fail not merely in execution but in conception: they treat explanation as an information-transfer problem while ignoring epistemic authority. The underlying assumption—that mathematical refinement can satisfy every stakeholder—is untenable. Useful explanations must balance multiple perspectives aiming for epistemic parity, a condition where diverse standpoints are given due weight. Yet when stakeholders request explanations, they often enter a hierarchy where technical authority dominates and other voices recede.

To address this imbalance, we propose **Domain Authority Negotiation (DAN)**—a framework that explicitly acknowledges conceptual misalignments and provides mechanisms for adjudicating competing institutional claims. Rather than seeking a universal standard for explanation, DAN frames interdisciplinary collaboration as an ongoing negotiation of authority across domains, where explanation—and other central concepts—emerge through the coordination of distinct forms of expertise. Only by confronting the epistemic power dynamics at the heart of collaboration can XAI move beyond its current impasse.

1.1 Related Work

Most influential XAI research defines explanation as a mathematical object—an entity with axioms, formal properties, and optimizable criteria [5,20,21,37,40,43]. This framing privileges logical soundness and tractability while sidelining social, legal, and ethical contexts. Yet such system-centered views overlook what makes explanations enlightening and actionable. This raises a critical question: Can a mathematically sanitized notion of explanation capture the complex, normative roles explanations play in science and society?

To further challenge this view, we briefly consider the philosophical question: **what is an explanation?** Simply put, explanations answer why something happens. There are at least two fundamental types of explanatory answers to'why' questions [36,48]. First, causal explanations trace the mechanisms that bring about a phenomenon—physical processes, computational operations, or environmental conditions producing an outcome. Second, intentional explanations account for behavior by detailing reasons, goals, or intentions—what agents aim to achieve given their beliefs and desires.

Both types may be relevant in XAI but are often conflated. Moreover, each type can be articulated at different levels. For example, a causal explanation of a model's output might range from high-level system's purpose, through specific procedures or models, down to physical or architectural details [23]. Similarly, intentional explanations in human-agent interaction can vary from detailed reasoning to general purpose summaries.

The nature of causality itself is complex and debated. Naïve monocausal models suggest single causes deterministically produce effects. While intuitive, this approach fails to capture real-world intricacies. More nuanced frameworks view causality as involving enabling and triggering conditions, where effects depend on groups of individually insufficient but non-redundant conditions, forming part of a collectively unnecessary but sufficient set of causes [22]. Contemporary discussions further emphasize causality's probabilistic nature, where causes increase outcome likelihood without guaranteeing it [3].

In XAI, what counts as a "cause" varies by context and theory, shaping explanations, fairness assessments, and trust. Crucially, an explanation's appropriateness depends on its intended purpose and must align with contextual needs [50]. Explanations serve diverse goals—from engineering debugging, to regulatory compliance, to encouraging trust in medical advice. Given AI's varied deployment contexts, this challenge is fundamental yet underappreciated.

This issue aligns closely with policy efforts such as the EU Guidelines for Trustworthy AI [7] and the AI Act [1], which emphasize transparency, human oversight, and stakeholder inclusion. These frameworks require that high-risk AI systems document their capabilities and limitations in accessible ways, reinforcing the need for explanations that are both meaningful and privacy-preserving across disciplines.

Research on differential privacy and feature-based XAI demonstrates that interpretability can coexist with data protection, though only through difficult trade-offs [12,33,41]. Explanations themselves, however, can expose sensitive details about model architectures and training data, turning transparency into a potential privacy vector [8]. Such risks are amplified in high-stakes domains where GDPR compliance intersects with the ethical dangers of surveillance misuse [49] and where latency and computational constraints hinder the deployment of privacy-aware XAI [13,27,32].

User-facing studies confirm that interpretability remains limited: even for simplified models, one-third of participants fail to use explanations effectively [25]. Emerging Explainable Interfaces (EIs) seek to improve communicative clarity [29], yet must also prevent leakage of model-specific information. These overlapping demands define a constrained design space in which clarity, privacy, and usability must be negotiated simultaneously.

Recent analyses highlight systemic problems in XAI. One paper identifies four: scope disagreements, definitional incoherence, problematic motivations, and inconsistent evaluation [47]. Another lists 28 open challenges for "XAI 2.0," including interdisciplinary integration and stakeholder adaptation [19]. Further,

Rudin argues that in high-stakes domains, post-hoc explanations should be abandoned in favor of inherently interpretable models [39].

While we share these diagnoses, our analysis differs in both cause and remedy. Where Rudin sees technical inadequacy, we identify conflicting authority frameworks. Even inherently interpretable models cannot reconcile what counts as valid explanation across domains. Calls for better interdisciplinary collaboration often mischaracterize these as "stakeholder needs"; we show they are competing epistemic claims that require institutional negotiation, not better design.

Most XAI research remains technically driven—only 7% of studies involve real-world domains [26]. Persistent problems include usability, cross-domain transfer, and fairness integration [8,30,42]. Addressing them demands genuinely interdisciplinary approaches combining computational rigor with non-technical insight.

Recent frameworks such as IDEP [2] propose structured approaches for domain-specific evaluation. Building on this direction, our study examines how experts from multiple fields jointly interpret XAI tools under privacy constraints. While such discussions are often framed at a high level of abstraction, their implications become most tangible when anchored in concrete cases where disciplinary logics meet. The following case of harbor front monitoring provides such an anchor, illustrating how technical, ethical, legal, and governance perspectives intersect in practice.

2 Case: Machine Unlearning in Harbor Front Monitoring

Below, we compare different disciplinary conceptualizations of a concrete, published example of XAI and examine the extent to which visualizations and metrics are considered explanatory from different perspectives. We focus on a recently published paper [46] that employs XAI techniques to explore"machine unlearning". The work focused on a use case in harbor front monitoring, where thermal cameras track and count various objects. The specific challenge was to explain an AI systems ability to forget how to categorize humans while maintaining its ability to identify other objects like vehicles and bicycles.

In this real-world application, the paper leveraged SIDU (Similarity Difference and Uniqueness) [24], an attribution-based XAI method, to verify the effectiveness of machine unlearning. SIDU generates heatmaps, visual representations that show which parts of an image the AI system pays attention to when making decisions, enabling the tracking of focus shifts after unlearning. From a technical perspective, these heatmaps revealed fascinating patterns: after unlearning, the system's attention was visibly shifted away from human patterns while maintaining focus on other objects (see Fig. 1).

To provide rigorous verification of the unlearning process, quantitative measures were developed. By introducing two complementary metrics—Heatmap Coverage (HC) and Attention Shift (AS)—the model quantitatively tracks the success of unlearning. Together, these metrics provide a quantitative means of verifying successful unlearning, complementing the qualitative insights from heatmap visualizations.

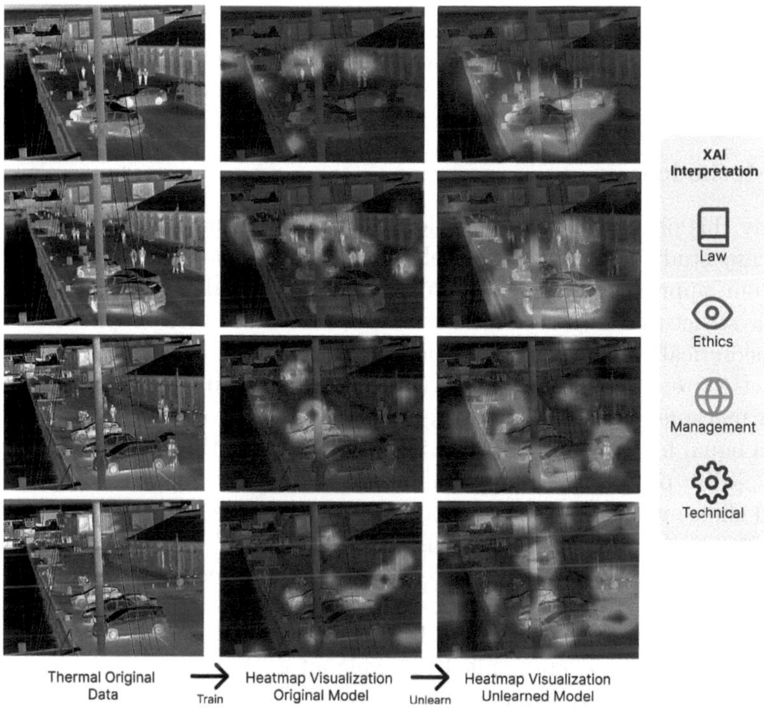

Fig. 1. Evolution of model attention patterns in privacy-preserving AI: from raw thermal harbor surveillance data (left), through GDPR-violating human detection (center, red regions indicating high attention), to unlearning of human patterns while preserving other detection capabilities (right). The first two rows illustrate a successful removal of attention of human patterns, while the last two rows indicate that the unlearned model is not properly forgetting the human related regions. (Color figure online)

The SIDU visualization method operates by computing attribution scores for each pixel in the input image, highlighting regions that significantly influence the model's decision. The HC metric quantifies spatial attention alignment by calculating the intersection between attention heatmaps and ground-truth object locations, while the AS metric measures the Euclidean distance between attention distributions before and after unlearning. In technical evaluations, successful unlearning was indicated by HC values decreasing significantly for human regions (average reduction of 62.3%) while remaining stable for non-human objects (average change of $\pm$ 7.5%), and AS values exceeding a threshold of 0.5 for images containing humans. From a computer vision perspective, these quantitative metrics provide mathematical rigor and meaningfully explain how the algorithm shifts its attention between different types of objects.

During discussions of this work in an interdisciplinary setting, however, a notable observation was made: while technical experts found the visualizations and metrics persuasive, experts in organizational studies, philosophy, and law deemed them far from convincing as tools of explanation. This aligns with previous research on misalignment between design intentions and actual stakeholder needs, e.g., [6,26].

2.1 Methodology

To study this phenomenon, we developed a mixed methods approach that combines case study analysis, expert elicitation, and comparative interpretation. While our approach is primarily qualitative, it provides empirical grounding through structured expert assessment of a real-world XAI application rather than theoretical conjecture. Consequently, this practice-based investigation captures active, real-world interpretative processes across disciplines.

Our methodological design deliberately places different disciplinary perspectives on equal footing—an explicit attempt to counter the epistemic hierarchies that typically privilege technical validation over other domains. This methodological choice itself represents a challenge to the implicit authority claims that shape interdisciplinary XAI research.

This approach follows a structured three-phase process:

1. **Case Selection and Analysis**: The case was selected as a concrete instance where XAI methods are applied for explanatory purposes.
2. **Expert Elicitation**: Domain experts were invited to evaluate the case example from their disciplinary perspective. Contributors were sampled based on established expertise in their respective fields and previous experience with the AI domain. Identical questions were posed to each expert to support comparability.
3. **Cross-disciplinary Comparative Analysis**: Responses were analyzed using a qualitative framework that examined (a) the conceptual role of explanations in each discipline, (b) criteria for evaluating XAI methods, and (c) identified gaps between technical capabilities and disciplinary requirements.

Specifically, we invited senior experts in organizational studies, law, and ethics—each engaged in interdisciplinary projects on responsible AI—to address the following research questions based on their close reading of the original XAI paper.

RQ1 What role do explanations play in your field?
RQ2 To what extent do the presented visualizations and metrics meet the criteria relevant to your discipline?
RQ3 What, if anything, is missing from these methods to make them valuable?

Each expert submitted a two-page response from their disciplinary perspective. The aim was proof of concept rather than statistical generalization: not to represent entire disciplines, but to demonstrate that different domains interpret identical XAI outputs through incompatible authority frameworks. Even a single clear case of such incompatibility suffices to establish the phenomenon. Variation within disciplines (e.g., privacy versus tort law, or organizational theory versus management science) reinforces rather than weakens the argument, showing that authority conflicts occur not only between but also within disciplines and institutional contexts. This nested structure makes the challenge more fundamental than mere interdisciplinary coordination. The conceptual contribution—reframing explanation from information transfer to authority negotiation—thus stands independently of sample size, addressing the structural logic of how domains validate knowledge claims.

Further, our analysis revealed that differences in writing style and academic orientation were not incidental but constitutive of each domain's epistemic authority. Analytical frameworks, evidentiary standards, and rhetorical strategies each embody distinct authority claims. We therefore reproduce the contributions in their original form, allowing readers to experience how these domain-specific modes of reasoning themselves articulate competing visions of what counts as an adequate explanation.

3 Results

This section presents our results, capturing how scholars from organizational studies, law, and ethics interpret XAI explanations in the context of the harbor front monitoring case. Following each contribution, we provide a brief interpretive commentary highlighting key disciplinary features and connections to the broader research questions.

Contributors were asked to limit their reflections to two pages, which is clearly a narrow space for such complex issues. Even so, the material provides rich insights, which we summarize and discuss below.

3.1 An Organizational Perspective

The following section is the third version received from the invited organizational studies team, upon clarification of what kind of response would be useful.

While the term "explainability" originates from technological disciplines, its interpretation and application have increasingly gained traction in organizational studies due to the "black box" concern about many AI systems with sensitive personal data [18]. *Explainability in technical research is primarily concerned with making AI systems' decision-making processes understandable to humans. Organizational studies adopt a broader lens on explainability that integrates technical transparency with concerns about governance, accountability, and ethical implications. Unlike the technical focus on algorithm optimization, organizational scholars view explainability as a mechanism for building trust within and outside organizational settings* [11]. *Organizational decision-makers must ensure that AI systems are not only technically explainable but also transparent in how decisions align with policies, public values, and legal standards. Hence, explainability in organizational contexts extends beyond technical experts to include multiple interests of stakeholders such as managers, regulators, employees, and end-users.*

Explainability can be viewed as a bridge between AI's technical and organizational/governance dimensions. As AI becomes increasingly central to decision-making, understanding and addressing this duality will be critical for organizations aiming to use AI responsibly and effectively. However, technical metrics of machine unlearning, heatmap visualizations, and the specific metrics HC & AS are not central to the discourse or research focus in organizational studies. From this perspective, their relevance depends, among other things, on whether stakeholders can understand the logic behind heatmap visualizations and the metrics and whether they align with organizational goals or values. Although the focus on developing AI systems that can forget or ignore specific information to support privacy protection and regulatory compliance appears relevant it is also "creating the risk that the explanations provided by XAI are not the kind required for governance" [4, p. 183].

In the concrete use case – AI and video technology for harbor monitoring – the relevance of the proposed unlearning verification and heatmap visualizations eventually depends on how they are perceived by key actors involved in the initiative including the rescue team and the police who on an everyday basis work with harbor safety and incidents, the municipality (who sponsored the initiative); researchers (who developed the algorithm for harbor safety), hardware and software providers, and citizens. However, when studying this case from an organizational perspective, technical issues about machine unlearning and heatmaps were outside the research focus [31]. *The researchers aimed to understand how AI-based public safety initiatives move from ideas in research labs to real-world operations through networks of heterogeneous actors. The study showed that although a shared objective of saving lives united the involved actors, the initiative was translated from ideas to an operational AI system through a slow-paced transformation where actors dealt with hopes, fears, setbacks, uncertainties, and renewed opportunities to move the initiative forward. While technical entities such as cameras, AI prototypes, and sensor technology were seen as crucial in this process* [31], *issues of unlearning verification and heatmap visualization were not included.*

Since machine unlearning and heatmap visualizations such as the metrics HC & AS are unfamiliar to organizational studies, interdisciplinary connections are needed to better understand their potential contributions. From an organizational perspective, these are some of the important questions:

1. *How can machine unlearning and heatmap visualizations contribute to operationalizing regulations like GDPR in practice, and what implications might this have for data security and privacy?*
2. *Who should have the right to decide what gets deleted in the context of machine unlearning? What power structures or gatekeepers do this create, and how might it potentially be misused in organizational contexts?*
3. *While machine unlearning and heatmap visualizations offer tools for implementing ethical principles, such as the "right to be forgotten", how do these tools work in real-world governance contexts, where political and economic constraints are present?*

4. *What unintended consequences might arise from machine unlearning and heatmap visualizations?*

To our knowledge, no one in organizational research has so far attempted to answer these questions. Organizational scholars, thus, currently have little to offer in terms of concrete guidelines or input for technical research or development in this context. Doing so would require closer interaction between computer science and organizational disciplines as well as analyses of concrete systems in specific application domains.

The response from the organizational perspective provides a compelling foundation for discussing explainability in XAI cases. The text notes that in scenarios such as harbor-front monitoring, explainability must serve a highly diverse group of stakeholders—including rescue teams, municipalities, researchers, industry, and citizens. Governance concerns, thus, extend far beyond algorithmic transparency to encompass policy alignment, decision authority, trust-building, and other factors.

Against this background, the text raises a hypothetical risk that XAI explanations may fall short of meeting all governance requirements but it does not explore how different stakeholders may have distinct needs for explanation.

Particularly interesting is the text's emphasis on explainability as a means of trust-building—something fundamentally different from explainability as a quantitative measure of attention shifts in AI models. However, this crucial disconnect is only implied rather than explicitly discussed. Furthermore, the text proposes a dynamic, process-oriented view of explainability—capturing hopes, fears, setbacks, uncertainties, and opportunities— which contrasts sharply with the static, technical approach commonly found in XAI research.

As such, while the heatmap study aimed to be useful for practitioners, the organizational studies response suggests that many key governance dimensions were overlooked. From this perspective, if the goal was practical relevance, the original study should have engaged more directly with real-world governance concerns.

Although the text does not explicitly address misalignment between XAI explanations and governance needs, it strongly implies that the relevance of heatmaps and machine unlearning in governance is limited at best. The text concludes with a series of broad questions for future research, but these are formulated so generally that they offer little concrete guidance for technical development.

Several aspects of the organizational studies contribution—e.g., the emphasis of stakeholder diversity, the orientation towards dynamical processes, the focus on trust and governance alignment—directly challenges the technical domain's assumption of epistemic primacy, positioning organizational acceptance as a prerequisite for deployment and more important than technical validation alone.

3.2 A Legal Perspective

The following section is the second version we received from the invited legal expert. It is a substantially rewritten version of the first draft we received.

In legal scholarship the terms "explainable" and "explainability" take on at least three distinct meanings depending on individual scholars' methodological outlook.

Most fundamentally, legal analysis is based on a distinction between "fact" and "law". A fact is a statement about some aspect of reality. In legal proceedings, fact is often established through a combination of methods – statements from witnesses or parties to the case, as well as various forms of supporting evidence, ranging from, e.g., background information about the issue at hand, to more technical and forensic materials, such as DNA analysis or fingerprints. As part of the latter, footage from CCTV cameras is increasingly used in legal proceedings, e.g., to identify individuals, their whereabouts or actions. Similarly, AI technologies are being used for law enforcement and evidential proceedings, e.g., to automatically track an individual's movement across multiple cameras, or to improve accuracy of facial recognitions [34]. *In the example used in this article, one could imagine XAI-based analysis of harbor front monitoring being used to help "explain" fact in different types of legal proceedings. For instance, a civil lawsuit might rely on this type of analysis to document individual risk behavior or lacking safeguards in a tort case.*

At a second level, explainability relates to the law side of the equation. The legal domain has traditionally been dominated by so-called doctrinal methods – in most parts of the world still the dominant approach to both university teaching and research [45]. *Doctrinal legal research (DLR) revolves around abductive and analogical reasoning, where the correct application of legal principles and ideas are abstracted and synthesized from a variety of sources, for instance case law or legal statutes. The exact scope of these sources and their mutual relationship depends on the specific jurisdiction and field of legal specialization. Yet, DLR differs from other types of social science research insofar as it aims towards particular and non-probabilistic statements of law, as opposed to more generalizable research findings* [10].

From this perspective, the kind of explanation that legal scholars and practitioners are concerned with is interpretive. Its aim is to distil what lawyers call "doctrine" – a set of truths accepted as authoritative. To do so, lawyers engage in a form of exegesis – a concept shared with law's theological roots, and which etymologically means exactly to explain by means of interpretation [28]. *Explainability in this sense therefore remains integral to all aspects of law. Law-making is the process of explaining historically God-given or custom-based, or today more often politically decided, written rules, i.e., by clarifying these rules and their authoritative interpretation. Explainability is vice versa a necessary quality for law to be law. A fundamental requirement for rules to be accepted as law is that they must be written or displayed so that their meaning is easily understood by those persons directly affected by them. And last, but not least, explainability is a basic requirement when applying law – a legal decision must be explained and reasoned in order to be legitimate and not appear arbitrary.*

The latter element, in particular, has gained particular importance in the context of AI-supported legal decision-making. As different forms of AI-supported or automated decision-making systems are increasingly utilizing large language models or other types of "black box" machine learning, concerns have been raised that such systems do not adhere to legal requirements for a right to an explanation. While not universally accepted and its exact scope still subject to debate, the right to (an) explanation has been codified in several jurisdictions. At the EU level, it follows from the 2016 General Data Protection Regulation (GDPR), which underscores that data subjects have the right "to obtain an explanation of the decision reached" (recital 71). More recently, the 2024 Artificial Intelligence Act (AI Act) provides a"right to explanation of individual decision-making" for high-risk systems which produce significant, adverse effects to an individual's health, safety or fundamental rights (Article 86).

Two opposed strategies exist for overcoming the explainability problem resulting from AI-supported legal decision-making. The first is legal and involves limiting AI-supported applications either based on pre-defined high-risk domains (as in the case of the EU AI Act) or on the basis of human-in-the-loop procedural requirements (as in the case of GDPR, which prohibits fully automated processing of personal information). The second is technical and aims to provide better explanations from existing algorithms, and algorithms that are more easily explainable – together dubbed Explainable AI (XAI). So far, however, applications of XAI in the legal domain remain limited, and no agreement exist on evaluation parameters for developing explainability acceptable to legal domain experts [38].

Third, and finally, recent years have seen a significant increase in more empirical legal studies (ELS), either seeking to complement or contrast doctrinal legal research. ELS have adopted a wide range of both qualitative and quantitative methods from other disciplines to the study of law and legal process. The meaning of explanation and explainability takes on different meanings depending on this methodological outlook. Qualitative empirical legal research will typically draw on interview data, observations and/or document analysis to provide explanations around how and why legal actors behave as they do, the operation of legal institutions (e.g., courts) or temporal shifts and developments in legal systems.

In recent years, a significant body of ELS have adopted more statistical and computational methods. Computational law aims to identify recursive patterns in legal materials by coding legal texts as data and analyzing these texts with algorithms. The majority of this work has thus far taken the form of coding written legal texts, such as judicial decisions, statutes, and international treaties, into a machine-readable form and then analyzing the texts on the basis of texts which is contained in the documents. Computational law thereby allows researchers to develop explanations that are more inductive, operate at a different scale, and offer a higher level of generalizability and controlled comparison than traditional methods.

As such, XAI as applied to law is uniquely suited to bridge the epistemological divide between doctrinal (DLR) and empirical (ELS) approaches marring the legal discipline. While most applications to date have been directed towards meeting legal requirements for explainability as part of automatization, XAI offers equally significant opportunities for application as part of empirical legal studies in terms of, for example, disclosing large-scale decision-making patterns that would elude individual, qualitative analysis, or identifying individual bias across multiple different dimensions. More concretely, techniques such as visual heatmapping have recently been pioneered in the legal domain – showing promise in terms highlighting relevant words or text passages relied upon by, e.g., large-language models as part of predicting legal outcomes [16]. *The particular value of such techniques speaks directly to both DLR and ELS agendas – on the one hand enabling legal domain experts to manually verify AI-supported recommender systems by directing them to relevant text bits within the input material, and on the other hand disclosing, e.g., bias if relevant input highlighted turns out to correlate with formally legally irrelevant factors.*

The response from the legal perspective is a superbly written and highly engaging text. Yet, although law as a discipline is closely tethered to ethical and procedural issues, the perspectives raised by the legal expert points to entirely different issues than those flagged in the ethical, organizational, and technical contributions. For example, when discussing the harbor-front case, the text focuses on tort law—specifically individual risk behaviors or the absence of adequate safeguards. In such contexts, 'unlearning' the ability to recognize humans appears not only irrelevant, but potentially counterproductive.

The text offers a clear analysis of the role of explanation in legal settings, revealing a fundamental misalignment between legal and technical notions of explanation. While XAI often seeks to enhance transparency through tools like heatmaps, legal requirements for explanation span at least three distinct levels: factual evidence, doctrinal interpretation, and empirical analysis. This discrepancy suggests that current XAI methods fall short of meeting legal standards, particularly under frameworks like the GDPR and the AI Act, which demand much more comprehensive justifications.

Although the text acknowledges the potential use of visualizations as evidence in legal proceedings, it does not directly engage with the harbor-front monitoring case or its associated privacy concerns. This omission highlights a broader gap between technical XAI solutions and the needs of legal practitioners operating in real-world contexts. That said, the response might have looked quite different had it come from a specialist in, for example, privacy law. Moreover, the text implies that effective legal XAI tools must go beyond visualizing model attention, to enable interpretation within established legal frameworks. This involves linking technical findings to legal principles and precedents—something current approaches have yet to achieve.

This implied requirement for legal interpretation represents a direct challenge to technical epistemic authority. The legal expert is not suggesting that technical explanations should be "improved" to better serve legal needs, but that legal interpretive frameworks should determine explanation adequacy—a fundamental authority claim that technical domains have largely ignored. Further, by invoking regulatory frameworks like GDPR and the AI Act, the legal expert leverages institutional authority to challenge technical validation—positioning legal compliance as non-negotiable and therefore taking precedence over technical criteria.

3.3 An Ethical Perspective

The following section is the original version we received from the invited ethics expert.

Imagine that a person after having traversed Aalborg Harbor is informed that thermal cameras were in place along the harbor front, and that the cameras are being used to make ML classifications of objects on the harbor front. The person is informed that he or she was classified as a 'human being'. Having been provided this information the person responds by posing a simple question: "Why was I classified as a human being?'

Assuming this to be a non-rhetorical question, the person is asking for an explanation. But what kind of explanation? Underlying the request for an explanation is an epistemic interest, i.e., an interest in getting some specific knowledge [35]. *The epistemic interest picks out some set of information about a situation as relevant for a person given his or her knowledge and wider interests and values. The epistemic interests concern a multitude of aspects of a situation some of which may be classified as 'non-ethics related' and some as 'ethics related.' The person posing the question 'why was I classified as a human being' may thus be asking for many different types of explanations.*

A non-ethics related epistemic interest could be philosophical in nature and concern the underlying model of 'humans' and 'persons.' The true meaning of the question 'why was I classified as a human being?' would therefore be something along the lines 'what are the distinctive features of a human being?' or 'what distinguishes a person from a human being?' The underlying epistemic interest could also be psychological in nature and concern the driving forces behind the tendency of people to make classifications of other people. The real question would therefore be 'what drives people to make classifications of others?' Also, the underlying interest could be technical and concern exactly what features of the thermal imaging that made the ML model make this classification. The corresponding reinterpretation of the question would consequently be 'what feature of the thermal images made the model classify me as a human being?' Additionally, the epistemic interest could also be directed at uncovering the commercial or public stakeholders facilitating the thermal camera classification of objects. The question would thus essentially be 'who is behind this implementation of thermal camera driven classification of objects on the harbor front?'

The epistemic interests inherent in the initial question 'why was I classified as a human being?' can also be ethics related. For present purposes, let us say that an epistemic interest is ethics related if it concerns information that is constitutive of or instrumental in protecting an individual against suffering harm or unfairness, or for protecting an individual's autonomy, privacy, dignity or some other relevant right (e.g., the right to an explanation), or for protecting other societal values such as transparency, trust, democracy, etc. To put it slightly differently, ethics related epistemic interests are interests in information and knowledge that we have ethical reasons for satisfying.

In the harbor case, the ethics related epistemic interests could originate in privacy concerns directly related to the classification of objects. The question 'why was I classified as a human being' would consequently be a question to the effect 'what—potentially personal and sensitive—information about me made it possible to classify me as a human being?" The question could also be related to the purpose of the classification, and the person's intention to 1) promote personal values related to that particular purpose, or 2) to protect him- or herself against potential harm and unfairness as well as autonomy and privacy violations following the use of thermal imaging for the purpose in question.

For the sake of argument, let us imagine that the purpose of using thermal cameras is to determine, on a daily basis, whether the level of human activity at the harbor justifies routine police patrols. Inquiring about the purpose of the classification would thus be relevant if a person believes thermal cameras to be a step in building an undesirable 'surveillance state' driven by commercial or political interests. It would also be relevant if a person is concerned that the system is inaccurate and biased in ways that is likely to result in fatal absence of police patrols on the harbor front and/or less safety for particular groups of people, i.e., discrimination.

The upshot of these considerations is simply this. There may be a multitude of epistemic interests underlying a simple request for an explanation of AI classification, and thus a multitude of explanations (and also explanation types). Some of these interests concern information and knowledge that is constitutive of and instrumental in protecting an individual's values, rights, and wider interests.

As previously outlined 'heatmaps' can be used to indicate which areas of an image that have been the most important for the classification of the image. Generally, this may aid a human interpreter, but may in certain circumstances also be misleading because the heatmap does not indicate which feature in the highlighted area that was important [9,35].

Imagine now that the person requesting an explanation for his or her classification as 'human being' is presented with a 'heatmap'. Would this empower the individual to take steps to avoid suffering harm, unfairness, privacy violations as well as protect and promote his or her wider interests? A 'heatmap' may certainly be relevant in assessing the risk of loss of privacy. If the heat map shows that areas of an image with people in it are of special importance for the classification of a person, then this could indicate that personal information is being processed as part of the classification.

Let us alter the initial scenario slightly to incorporate the idea of privacy preserving AI. Imagine now that the person traversing the harbor is informed that thermal cameras have provided input to a classification of objects other than humans, and that the person is provided a 'heatmap' showing that no areas of a thermal image with people in it were used for the classification. Clearly this would be relevant for an assessment of the privacy violation. If no areas of a thermal image with people in it is being used for the classification of objects, then it seems hard pressed to claim that the classification violates privacy in the sense that it processes personal or sensitive information.

However, as our considerations in the previous sections have shown, the epistemic interests that may drive a request for an explanation are many and diverse. Narrowing the scope to ethics related epistemic interests does not change the picture. As an explanation, 'heatmaps' does little to satisfy individuals' ethics related epistemic interests, i.e., it does not empower individuals to protect themselves against using thermal imaging on the harbor front for purposes leading to discrimination and violating other deeply held values and interests. In short, 'heatmaps' have very limited value as a type of explanation that serves to satisfy ethics related epistemic interests.

Needless to say, our considerations in this section may have little bearing on whether to use thermal imaging for various purposes on any given harbor front. It has focused entirely on the potential of 'heatmaps' for satisfying ethics related epistemic interests.

The response from the ethical perspective is, once again, highly engaging and thought-provoking, but also clearly differs in academic style, focus, and basic assumptions from the other contributions. The text centrally employs one of the most established tools in analytical philosophy: the thought experiment. By inviting the reader to imagine a series of hypothetical scenarios, it systematically unpacks the epistemic interests that may underlie a seemingly simple request for an explanation. Crucially, it shows how highly technical explanation methods, such as heatmaps, fail to connect with broader ethical concerns, perhaps in part because their quantitative nature is ill-suited to the kind of imaginative engagement that ethical inquiry requires.

In our reading, a key contribution of the text is its distinction between ethics-related and non-ethics-related epistemic interests in explanations—a distinction that fundamentally challenges the relevance of many current XAI approaches for most practical concerns. Through the harbor front case, the text illustrates how explanations serve different purposes depending on the epistemic interests at stake. While technical methods may satisfy a general curiosity about model behavior, they fall short of addressing ethical concerns related to privacy, surveillance, discrimination, and power dynamics.

The text defines ethics-related epistemic interests as involving"information that is constitutive of or instrumental in protecting an individual against suffering harm or unfairness, or for protecting an individual's autonomy, privacy, dignity, or some other relevant right (e.g., the right to an explanation), or for protecting other societal values such as transparency, trust, democracy, etc." Against this backdrop, heatmaps appear to have very limited value in meeting such epistemic interests. Even when they successfully indicate that human-related features were not used in classification—thereby suggesting some degree of privacy preservation—they offer little insight into the broader ethical stakes of AI decision-making.

The discussion suggests that meaningful ethical explanations should empower individuals to act upon the information they receive—to protect themselves from harm or injustice. By this standard, current XAI techniques fall far short. Obviously, this does not imply that they are entirely without value, but it underscores the need for XAI developers to be cautious in overestimating the relevance of technical explanations for addressing non-technical concerns.

The emphasis on empowerment constitutes an implicit authority claim—one that holds explanations should be judged by their capacity to enable human agency, rather than by their mathematical or statistical properties. By foregrounding empowerment, the ethicist elevates ethical evaluation above technical validation. Moreover, the use of philosophical tools—especially the thought experiment—reinforces this stance methodologically: it implicitly asserts that conceptual analysis, not computational precision, is the appropriate means for assessing explanation adequacy. In privileging human reasoning over algorithmic behavior, the ethicist challenges the technical domain's claim to set the standard for what counts as a meaningful explanation.

4 Discussion

We note that while there is general agreement on the importance of explanations (RQ1), significant disparities emerge in how each discipline evaluate XAI tools (RQ2). Notably, all disciplines identify critical missing elements (RQ3) that must be addressed for XAI to be valuable in their respective domains. This comparison highlights the need for far more integrated approaches that can bridge the technical-practical gap while satisfying diverse stakeholder requirements.

Although all three perspectives agree that explainability must go beyond mere technical transparency, they diverge on what should take its place. For organizations, the priority is aligning AI systems with internal governance objectives; for law, it is ensuring compliance with pre-existing legal frameworks that operate hierarchically—often extending far beyond the specifics of the case at hand; and for ethics, it is empowering individuals to protect their rights and values. The analysis thus reveals not only a gap between technical outputs and stakeholder needs, but also fundamental divergences among the perspectives themselves over what should replace the technical paradigm as primary. In our view, these gaps are not simply matters of informational mismatch, but manifestations of unresolved authority struggles: each domain implicitly rejects others' authority to determine what constitutes proper explanation.

A recurring theme is the lack of meaningful collaboration between disciplines. Organizational research calls for input from computer science to develop practical tools; legal scholarship seeks greater integration of empirical methodologies; and ethical inquiry demands a more holistic approach to XAI—one that bridges technical and societal dimensions. These interdisciplinary gaps are central to the challenge of making XAI genuinely useful. Yet bridging them requires more than improved technical methods or closer collaboration. It calls for explicit mechanisms to negotiate competing claims to epistemic authority, acknowledging that no single domain holds inherent primacy over the others.

While the different disciplines agree that current XAI approaches fall short, they also concur that the path forward lies in interdisciplinary collaboration rather than in any one field monopolizing the development of operational XAI. This consensus on collaboration masks a deeper question that remains unaddressed, however: who decides what counts as valid explanation? Without explicitly acknowledging and negotiating competing authority claims, calls for collaboration often reproduce existing epistemic hierarchies that privilege technical validation over other domains. Such collaboration will inevitably confront authority questions: Whose standards determine whether an explanation is "good enough"? How are conflicts between technical accuracy and organizational utility resolved? Who has final validation authority when domains disagree?

While our analysis centers on the harbor front monitoring case, the cross-disciplinary conceptual and authority misalignments we identify likely extend to other domains where XAI intersects with regulatory and ethical concerns, such as healthcare, finance, and autonomous transportation.

4.1 The Domain Authority Negotiation Framework

In response, we propose Domain Authority Negotiation (DAN) as a radical alternative framework that explicitly acknowledges and addresses the epistemic power dynamics inherent in interdisciplinary collaboration. In our example of XAI, rather than asking "How can we make this model transparent?" DAN poses three questions that current XAI frameworks systematically avoid:

1. Who should have validation authority over different aspects of AI systems?
2. How should conflicts between authority domains be resolved?
3. What institutional mechanisms are needed to negotiate authority boundaries?

DAN is founded on four elements that fundamentally challenge current XAI assumptions:

1. **Authority Domain Mapping:** Identifies which domains hold legitimate authority over different aspects of an AI system. In the harbor monitoring case, for example, technical experts have authority over computational efficiency and model performance; legal experts over GDPR compliance and evidence standards; organizational stakeholders over alignment with operational procedures; and ethicists over privacy protection and the ethical use of data.
2. **Explicit Authority Boundaries:** Clearly defines the scope and limits of authority across domains. For instance, legal experts may have primary authority over personal data handling under GDPR, with technical and ethical experts serving in consultative roles. Conversely, technical experts may

lead decisions on model architecture, while legal and ethical domains retain notification or advisory input.
3. **Negotiation Mechanisms:** Establishes formal processes for managing authority claims across domains. These include:
   - ***Cross-Domain Translation Protocols***: Structured procedures for articulating concerns in domain-relevant language.
   - ***Authority Dispute Resolution:*** Mechanisms for adjudicating conflicting authority claims.
   - ***Boundary Objects:*** Shared artifacts for cross-domain intepretation, enabling coordination without consensus.
4. **Formalized Institutional Structures:** Sustained authority negotiation depends on formal institutional support. The framework calls for:
   - ***Authority Councils:*** Groups with representatives from each domain to oversee authority allocation and disputes.
   - ***Negotiation Protocols:*** Clearly documented procedures for raising, discussing, and resolving authority-related conflicts.
   - ***Dynamic Adjustment Mechanisms:*** Processes for revising authority boundaries in response to system evolution or contextual change.

While full operationalization requires empirical piloting beyond this paper's scope, several feasible implementation pathways can be outlined. DAN could be introduced through: (1) small-scale institutional experiments where organizations deploying high-stakes AI test limited Authority Councils on concrete disputes; (2) regulatory sandboxes that let authorities and developers trial DAN-based governance under supervised conditions; (3) professional society initiatives developing model negotiation protocols for domains such as healthcare or finance; and (4) academic–industry partnerships documenting authority conflicts in real deployments. Each pathway would yield evidence on DAN's relevance and effectiveness, organizational overhead, and its potential to democratize—or inadvertently entrench—existing power structures, a risk that requires explicit safeguards in implementation.

DAN represents more than an incremental improvement: it reconceptualizes explanation itself—from information transfer to authority negotiation. Rather than asking why legal experts find technical heatmaps inadequate, DAN reframes heatmaps as instruments of technical authority and calls for distinct artifacts for legal authority functions, linked through negotiated interfaces instead of assumed translatability.

Practically, this means developing models that recognize domain boundaries and invoke appropriate validation frameworks. When processing legally sensitive features, for example, a system would not produce a heatmap hoping it satisfies legal standards but would activate a specialized legal validation module applying doctrinal interpretation frameworks directly. This shift—from monolithic explanations to modular validation systems—allows different parts of a decision to be explained through domain-specific protocols with explicit handoffs across authority boundaries. Far from diminishing technical XAI, this approach demands more sophisticated designs embedding domain knowledge and authority relations into the system architecture.

Applied to the harbor monitoring case, DAN would transform how privacy is managed. Rather than relying on heatmaps to verify GDPR compliance in machine unlearning, the system would combine technical evaluation metrics (e.g., HC and AS) with legal, organizational, and ethical validation layers. When processing human images, the system would automatically trigger legal and ethical protocols instead of translating technical outputs for those domains—preventing the misalignments observed in cross-domain evaluations. The resulting governance structure would strengthen accountability, protect privacy rights, and better integrate surveillance into public safety operations.

DAN's implications extend well beyond the case of explanation in XAI. In healthcare, diagnostic algorithms face similar challenges in meeting clinical, legal, and ethical standards; DAN could clarify authority boundaries among medical expertise, patient rights, regulatory oversight, and institutional governance. Yet without careful design, it could also reinforce existing medical hierarchies. The same tension applies to finance, criminal justice, and autonomous systems: DAN can either democratize AI governance by making authority explicit and negotiable or reinforce entrenched power by codifying it. The outcome depends on how authority negotiations are structured—whether they establish genuine epistemic parity or merely formalize dominance.

Ultimately, implementing DAN means recognizing that authority is distributed. Technical validation, legal compliance, organizational governance, and ethical reasoning are each legitimate and necessary forms of validation that must be coordinated rather than hierarchically ordered. The artifacts of explanation—technical visualizations, legal documentation, organizational procedures, ethical analyses—must be designed not just for internal clarity but for deliberate coordination across domains. Doing so will require sustained institutional forums where experts from these domains negotiate and tailor authority boundaries in concrete applications, moving from translation to genuine collaboration.

5 Conclusion

This paper has argued that entrenched epistemic hierarchies lie at the root of the conceptual misalignments between technical approaches to explanation and the demands of legal, organizational, and ethical domains. Bridging this gap requires more than technical refinement—it demands a shift in how explanatory authority is defined, distributed, and negotiated. If explanations are to serve real-world needs, they must move beyond notions of technical transparency to embody contextual relevance, human interpretability, and normative alignment.

Technical authority often manifests in practices that privilege quantitative over qualitative reasoning, demand mathematical formalization even when it obscures meaning, and treat transparency as the ultimate measure of trustworthiness. Other domains assert competing claims, producing a contested explanatory landscape where what counts as a good explanation depends less on clarity or utility than on whose standards of authority prevail.

Although the potential benefits of genuine interdisciplinary integration are clear, structural and epistemic barriers continue to hinder it. The present analysis exposes misalignments that could, in principle, be mitigated through sustained efforts at mutual understanding. Yet doing so would require a willingness to negotiate—and at times compromise—positions within existing hierarchies of expertise. Only through deliberate authority design can AI systems become accountable to the full range of human concerns they affect.

Looking forward, key opportunities that DAN opens for the XAI field include:

1. Domain-specific explanation modules that recognize authority boundaries.
2. Formal boundary objects for cross-domain interpretation without assuming direct translation.
3. Institutional structures supporting ongoing authority negotiation in AI deployment.
4. Evaluation metrics for explanation effectiveness while accounting for authority differences.
5. Curricula for AI practitioners focused on epistemic authority dynamics, not just technical explanations.
6. Stronger engagement with policy frameworks such as the EU AI Act, focusing on authority distribution rather than generic transparency

These opportunities represent more than incremental improvements to current XAI practice. They call for a reconceptualization of what explanation means in AI contexts and how it can serve diverse stakeholders without assuming universal translatability.

Several limitations of this study indicate directions for future work. Our empirical demonstration, based on three domain experts and a single case study, provides proof of concept but not generality. Broader empirical studies are needed to map authority conflicts across domains and applications. The DAN framework also remains conceptual; its operationalization will require institutional experimentation to identify effective governance structures, resource requirements, and safeguards against reproducing existing hierarchies. While this study focused on XAI in surveillance and monitoring, authority conflicts in other high-stakes domains—such as healthcare, finance, and criminal justice—deserve further investigation. Moreover, because the analysis centers on Western institutional contexts, future research should explore how epistemic authority operates across different cultural and legal traditions.

Future research should thus include systematic mapping of authority conflicts across AI domains, empirical pilots of DAN-based governance models, cross-cultural studies of epistemic authority, and longitudinal analyses of how authority negotiation evolves as AI systems become embedded in institutional decision-making. Together, these efforts might refine our understanding of when and how explicit authority negotiation can enhance AI governance and contribute to genuinely accountable, context-aware systems.

Acknowledgments. This research is supported by the Grundfos Foundation ("REPAI", grant no. 83648813); Independent Research Fund Denmark ("Contestable

Artificial Intelligence", grant no. 10.46540/2027-00140B); Danish National Research Foundation (grant no. DNRF169, Center of Excellence for Global Mobility Law); and Villum Foundation ("XAI-CRED", grant no. 69198).

References

1. Regulation (EU) 2024/1689 of the European Parliament and of the Council of 13 June 2024 laying down harmonised rules on artificial intelligence and amending Regulations (EC) No 300/2008, (EU) No 167/2013, (EU) No 168/2013, (EU) 2018/858, (EU) 2018/1139 and (EU) 2019/2144 and Directives 2014/90/EU, (EU) 2016/797 and (EU) 2020/1828 (Artificial Intelligence Act) (2024)
2. Bennett, C.R.e.a.: Interdisciplinary Expertise to Advance Equitable Explainable AI (2024). https://arxiv.org/abs/2406.18563
3. Cartwright, N.: The dappled world: a study of the boundaries of science. Cambridge University Press (1999)
4. Danks, D.: Governance via explainability. In: Bullock, J.B., et al. (eds.) The Oxford Handbook of AI Governance, pp. 183–197 (2022). https://doi.org/10.1093/oxfordhb/9780197579329.013.11
5. Díaz-Rodríguez, N., Del Ser, J., Coeckelbergh, M., de Prado, M.L., Herrera-Viedma, E., Herrera, F.: Connecting the dots in trustworthy artificial intelligence: from AI principles, ethics, and key requirements to responsible ai systems and regulation. Inf. Fusion **99**, 101896 (2023)
6. Ehsan, U., Passi, S., Liao, Q., Chan, L., Lee, I., Muller, M., Riedl, M.: The who in XAI: how AI background shapes perceptions of AI explanations. In: Proceedings of the CHI Conference on Human Factors in Computing Systems, pp. 1–32 (2024)
7. European Commission and Directorate-General for Communications Networks, Content and Technology and Grupa ekspertów wysokiego szczebla ds. sztucznej inteligencji: ethics guidelines for trustworthy AI. Publications Office (2019). https://doi.org/10.2759/346720
8. Ezzeddine, F.: Privacy implications of explainable AI in data-driven systems. In: Proceedings of the 2024 International Conference on AI and Data Engineering, pp. 361–368 (2024). https://doi.org/10.48550/arXiv.2406.15789
9. Ghassemi, M., Oakden-Rayner, L., Beam, A.L.: The false hope of current approaches to explainable artificial intelligence in health care. Lancet Digit. Heal. **3**(11), e745–e750 (2021)
10. Goodrich, P.: Historical aspects of legal interpretation. Indiana Law J. **61**, 331 (1985)
11. Grimmelikhuijsen, S.: Explaining why the computer says no: Algorithmic transparency affects the perceived trustworthiness of automated decision-making. Public Adm. Rev. **83**(2), 241–262 (2023). https://doi.org/10.1111/puar.13483
12. Harder, F., Bauer, M., Park, M.: Interpretable and differentially private predictions. ArXiv abs/1906.02004 (2019). https://doi.org/10.1609/AAAI.V34I04.5827
13. Huong, T.T., Ta, P.B., Kieu, H.D., Hoang, N.V., N., H., Hung, N.T., K., T.: Federated learning-based explainable anomaly detection for industrial control systems. IEEE Access (2022). https://doi.org/10.1109/ACCESS.2022.3173288
14. Hvidtfeldt, R.: The Structure of Interdisciplinary Science. NDPS, Springer, Cham (2018). https://doi.org/10.1007/978-3-319-90872-4_9
15. Hvidtfeldt, R., Pedersen, D.B.: On conceptual entropy: Metaphors We Die From. Dan. Yearb. Philos. **57**(1), 116–133 (2024)

16. Jahromi, M.N., et al.: SIDU-TXT: an XAI algorithm for NLP with a holistic assessment approach. Nat. Language Process. J. **7**, 100078 (2024)
17. Kuhn, T.S.: The structure of scientific revolutions. chicago: Univ. Press, Chicago (1962)
18. Lebovitz, S., Lifshitz-Assaf, H., Levina, N.: To engage or not to engage with AI for critical judgments: how professionals deal with opacity when using AI for medical diagnosis. Organ. Sci. **33**(1), 126–148 (2022)
19. Longo, L., Brcic, M., et al.: Explainable Artificial Intelligence (XAI) 2.0: a manifesto of open challenges and interdisciplinary research directions. Inf. Fusion **106**, 102301 (2024). https://doi.org/10.1016/j.inffus.2024.102301
20. Lundberg, S.M., Lee, S.I.: A unified approach to interpreting model predictions. Adv. Neural Inf. Process. Syst. **30** (2017)
21. Lyu, Q., Apidianaki, M., Callison-Burch, C.: Towards faithful model explanation in NLP: a survey. Comput. Linguist. **50**(2), 657–723 (2024)
22. Mackie, J.L.: The cement of the universe: a study of causation. Clarendon Press (1980)
23. Marr, D.: Vision: a computational investigation into the human representation and processing of visual information. MIT Press (2010)
24. Muddamsetty, S.M., Jahromi, M.N., Ciontos, A.E., Fenoy, L.M., Moeslund, T.B.: Visual explanation of black-box model: Similarity Difference and Uniqueness (SIDU) method. Pattern Recogn. **127**, 108604 (2022)
25. Narayanan, M., Chen, E., He, J., Kim, B., Gershman, S., Doshi-Velez, F.: How do humans understand explanations from machine learning systems? an evaluation of the human-interpretability of explanation. arXiv preprint arXiv:1802.00682 (2018)
26. Naveed, S., Stevens, G., Robin-Kern, D.: An overview of the empirical evaluation of explainable AI (XAI): a comprehensive guideline for user-centered evaluation in XAI. Appl. Sci. **14**(23), 11288 (2024)
27. Nazat, S., Arreche, O., Abdallah, M.: On evaluating black-box explainable AI methods for enhancing anomaly detection in autonomous driving systems. Sensors **24** (2024). https://doi.org/10.3390/s24113515
28. Neoh, J.: Text, doctrine and tradition in law and religion. Oxford J. Law Religion **2**(1), 175–199 (2013)
29. Nguyen, T., Canossa, A., Zhu, J.: How human-centered explainable AI interfaces are designed and evaluated: a systematic survey. arXiv preprint arXiv:2403.14496 (2024)
30. Nguyen, T., Huynh, T., et al.: A survey of privacy-preserving model explanations: privacy risks, attacks, and countermeasures. ArXiv (2024). https://doi.org/10.48550/arXiv.2404.00673
31. Noesgaard, M., Nielsen, J., Nørgaard, S.: Making society a safer place through artificial intelligence: the slow-paced transition from idea to sustainable solution. In: ICIS 2024 Proceedings. No. 26 (2024). https://aisel.aisnet.org/icis2024/aiinbus/aiinbus/26
32. Ogrezeanu, I., et al.: Privacy-preserving and explainable AI in industrial applications. Appl. Sci. (2022). https://doi.org/10.3390/app12136395
33. Patel, N., Shokri, R., Zick, Y.: Model explanations with differential privacy. In: Proceedings of the 2022 ACM Conference on Fairness, Accountability, and Transparency (2020). https://doi.org/10.1145/3531146.3533235
34. Pisati, R., Astya, R., Chauhan, P.: A profound review of AI-driven crime detection in CCTV videos. In: 2024 Sixth International Conference on Computational Intelligence and Communication Technologies (CCICT). IEEE (2024)

35. Ploug, T., Holm, S.: The limits of explainability in health AI - why current concepts of AI explainability cannot accommodate patient interests. J. Appl. Ethics Philosophy (2025)
36. Randolph Mayes, G.: Theories of explanation. In: Fieser, J. (ed.) Internet Encyclopedia of Philosophy. https://iep.utm.edu/explanat/
37. Ribeiro, M.T., Singh, S., Guestrin, C.: " why should i trust you?" explaining the predictions of any classifier. In: Proceedings of the 22nd ACM SIGKDD International Conference on Knowledge Discovery and Data Mining, pp. 1135–1144 (2016)
38. Richmond, K.M., et al.: Explainable AI and law: an evidential survey. Digital Soc. **3**(1), 1 (2024)
39. Rudin, C.: Stop explaining black box machine learning models for high stakes decisions and use interpretable models instead. Nat. Mach. Intell. **1**(5), 206–215 (2019). https://doi.org/10.1038/s42256-019-0048-x
40. Saeed, W., Omlin, C.: Explainable AI (XAI): a systematic meta-survey of current challenges and future opportunities. Knowl.-Based Syst. **263**, 110273 (2023)
41. Saifullah, S., Mercier, D., Lucieri, A., Dengel, A., Ahmed, S.: The privacy-explainability trade-off: unraveling the impacts of differential privacy and federated learning on attribution methods. Front. Artif. Intell. **7** (2022). https://doi.org/10.3389/frai.2024.1236947
42. Schmidt, J., Pietsch, V., Nocker, M., Rader, M., Montuoro, A.: Navigating the trade-off between explainability and privacy. In: Proceedings of the 2024 International Conference on Data Engineering, pp. 726–733 (2024). https://doi.org/10.5220/0012472200003660
43. Selvaraju, R.R., Cogswell, M., Das, A., Vedantam, R., Parikh, D., Batra, D.: Grad-cam: Visual explanations from deep networks via gradient-based localization. In: Proceedings of the IEEE International Conference on Computer Vision, pp. 618–626 (2017)
44. Shapin, S., Schaffer, S.: Leviathan and the air-pump: Hobbes, Boyle, and the experimental life. Princeton University Press (2011)
45. Varuhas, J.N.E.: Mapping doctrinal methods. In: Daly, P., Tomlinson, J. (eds.) Researching Public Law in Common Law Systems. Edward Elgar, Cheltenham (2023)
46. Vidal, À.P., Johansen, A.S., Jahromi, M.N.S., Escalera, S., Nasrollahi, K., Moeslund, T.B.: Verifying Machine Unlearning with Explainable AI. In: Palaiahnakote, S., Schuckers, S., Ogier, JM., Bhattacharya, P., Pal, U., Bhattacharya, S. (eds) Pattern Recognition. ICPR 2024 International Workshops and Challenges. ICPR 2024. LNCS, vol 15619. Springer, Cham (2025). https://doi.org/10.1007/978-3-031-88223-4_32
47. Weber, R.O., Johs, A.J., Goel, P., Silva, J.M.: XAI is in trouble. AI Mag. **45**(3), 300–316 (2024)
48. Woodward, J., Ross, L.: Scientific explanation. In: Zalta, E.N. (ed.) The Stanford Encyclopedia of Philosophy. Metaphysics Research Lab, Stanford University, summer 2021 edn. (2021). https://plato.stanford.edu/archives/sum2021/entries/scientific-explanation/
49. Yew, R.J., Qin, L., Venkatasubramanian, S.: You still see me: How data protection supports the architecture of ML surveillance. ArXiv **abs/2402.06609** (2024). https://doi.org/10.48550/arXiv.2402.06609
50. Zablocki, É., Ben-Younes, H., Pérez, P., Cord, M.: Explainability of deep vision-based autonomous driving systems: review and challenges. Int. J. Comput. Vision **130**(10), 2425–2452 (2022). https://doi.org/10.48550/arXiv.2101.05307

Linking Architectural Threat Modeling of AI Systems to MITRE ATLAS via Semantic Knowledge Graphs

Joakim Rosell(✉), Maria Ulan, and Max Fransson

RISE Research Institutes of Sweden, Lindholmspiren 7A, 417 56 Gothenburg, Sweden
{joakim.rosell,maria.ulan,max.fransson}@ri.se

Abstract. This paper demonstrates how semantic knowledge graph integration can bridge organizational threat modeling and adversarial frameworks for responsible AI security assessment. We applied ThreatFinder.ai to an AI-based facial anonymization system, identifying 12 assets, 33 instantiated threats (7 unique), and 157 instantiated controls (28 unique). These outputs were transformed into knowledge graphs and semantically linked to MITRE ATLAS using Sentence-BERT embeddings, creating explicit, auditable mappings between organizational threats and adversarial techniques. The linking produced 123 `threat→technique`, 72 `threat→SubTechnique`, and 21 `control→mitigation` alignments (covering 55 unique threats and 15 unique controls), enabling asset-centric reasoning and transparent security decision-making. The methodology satisfies multiple stakeholder needs: organizational usability through familiar workflows, governance compliance through auditable relations, and ethical transparency through accessible visualizations. These results show that interdisciplinary requirements can drive approaches to AI security that are both technically rigorous and practically usable.

Keywords: AI security · Threat modeling · Semantic knowledge graphs · Adversarial ML · Responsible AI

1 Introduction

AI security assessments fail when approached from a single discipline. Technical frameworks produce adversarial insights inaccessible to decision-makers, while organizational risk methods lack technical depth, creating a false sense of confidence. Governance frameworks emphasize explainability and transparency but often lack concrete audit mechanisms to verify compliance. These failures are structural: each discipline optimizes for its own goals, but AI security requires simultaneous alignment across technical rigor, organizational adoption, and governance compliance.

Current AI security frameworks illustrate the limitations of single-discipline approaches. MITRE ATLAS [15] provides comprehensive adversarial knowledge,

K. Nasrollahi et al. (Eds.): REPAI-W 2025, LNCS 16390, pp. 24–40, 2026.
https://doi.org/10.1007/978-3-032-16886-3_2

ENISA offers systematic threat landscape analysis [5], and OWASP provides practical engineering guidelines [17]. Each represents state-of-the-art understanding within its disciplinary focus, yet organizational research reveals that practitioners abandon tools requiring specialized adversarial ML expertise [8,16]. In contrast, tools such as ThreatFinder.ai [2,3] achieve high usability through asset-centric workflows, but constrain technical depth: their internal ATLAS integration remains implicit within the tool and not externally auditable, preventing advanced threat analysis. In this study, we demonstrate our methodology using an AI-driven facial anonymization pipeline that maintains behavioral attributes (such as gaze and expression) while removing identity cues to meet GDPR requirements. The system architecture follows the design principles of recent frameworks like FaceDancer [21], and includes components for face detection, identity encoding, and anonymized-face synthesis.

These tensions create concrete design constraints. The EU AI Act[1] and GDPR[2] demand explainable logic for automated decision-making in high-risk systems, eliminating black-box approaches while requiring technical sophistication beyond typical organizational capabilities. Cognitive load research constrains visualization complexity to 7 ± 2 relationships [13]. Governance auditability requires explicit, queryable relationships over implicit embeddings. Existing approaches fail because technical optimization for algorithmic performance produces organizationally unusable systems [11,14].

We address this by transforming ThreatFinder.ai [3] threat models into knowledge graphs and semantically linking them to MITRE ATLAS using Sentence-BERT embeddings [18]. When applied in the context of facial anonymization, we identified 123 `threat→technique` mappings, 72 `threat→SubTechnique` mappings, and 21 `control→mitigation` alignments (covering 55 unique threats and 15 unique controls). This integration enables asset-centric reasoning and transparent security decision-making: organizational workflows are preserved, auditability is ensured, and visualizations remain cognitively accessible. The results demonstrate how interdisciplinary requirements can drive technical innovations that single-discipline approaches cannot achieve.

2 Background and Related Work

The deployment of AI systems is increasingly framed within *responsible AI*, emphasizing technical robustness alongside ethical, legal, and organizational accountability. Security is central to this responsibility: adversarial manipulation of AI models can undermine safety, fairness, and trust. AI Trust, Risk, and Security Management (AI TRiSM[3]) [7] has emerged as a unifying approach across the AI lifecycle, promoting transparency, monitoring, and secure model operations. However, adoption faces challenges including adversarial vulnerabilities, regulatory gaps, and skill shortages, underscoring the need for methods

[1] Regulation (EU) 2024/1689, https://eur-lex.europa.eu/eli/reg/2024/1689/oj.
[2] Regulation (EU) 2016/679, https://eur-lex.europa.eu/eli/reg/2016/679/oj.
[3] AI TRiSM, https://www.gartner.com/en/articles/ai-trust-and-ai-risk.

that connect threats to both technical and organizational controls. Advances in semantic embedding models (e.g., Sentence-BERT) [18] enable alignment of heterogeneous security taxonomies through semantic similarity rather than rigid keyword rules, motivating our approach.

Several complementary frameworks address AI-specific security concerns. The European Union Agency for Cybersecurity (ENISA) publishes recurring threat landscape reports highlighting the evolving risks to AI and digital infrastructure [5]. The OWASP AI Security & Privacy Guide provides practical engineering guidelines, offering mitigation strategies and concrete security controls tailored to AI development and deployment; many of these controls are incorporated in the ThreatFinder taxonomy used in this work [17]. The MITRE ATLAS framework (Adversarial Threat Landscape for Artificial-Intelligence Systems) extends the widely-used ATT&CK model into the AI domain by documenting tactics, techniques, SubTechniques, mitigations, and real-world case studies of adversarial behavior [15]. ATLAS has been positioned as state-of-the-art for adversarial knowledge [1] and empirically evaluated for effectiveness against concrete attacks such as data poisoning [26]. Maintained as a living knowledge base and published in structured JSON format, ATLAS is suitable for integration into knowledge graph representations. Surveys of AI security threats catalogue common attack vectors, including data poisoning, adversarial examples, model inversion, evasion, and model extraction [8]. Combined, these sources highlight the breadth of the AI threat landscape and motivate the need for methods that connect threats to defenses and organizational responses.

In our work, MITRE ATLAS serves as the adversarial reference layer. We construct a dedicated knowledge graph representation of ATLAS (the *ATLAS Graph*, ATG) from its JSON files, which allows us to explicitly link organizational threats elicited through ThreatFinder.ai with adversarial tactics and techniques documented in ATLAS. This separation—ATLAS as a reference framework and ATG as our graph instantiation—ensures that our methodology remains reproducible and transparent while enabling explainable cross-layer reasoning between organizational and adversarial perspectives.

Translating framework knowledge into system-specific threat models remains difficult. General tools (e.g., Microsoft TMT[4], CAIRIS[5], ThreatSpec[6]) lack AI-specific taxonomies and require substantial manual effort [3]. ThreatFinder.ai addresses this gap through an asset-centric approach to AI threat modeling and risk assessment. It integrates knowledge from ENISA, the OWASP AI Security & Privacy Guide, and MITRE ATLAS into a graph-based meta-model that guides analysts through asset elicitation, automated threat identification, control assignment, and subsequent business impact analysis and Monte Carlo-based risk quantification [2,3]. Building on this foundation, our work externalizes ThreatFinder.ai outputs into a knowledge graph representation to enable explainable, cross-layer reasoning that connects system-specific threats to adver-

[4] https://www.microsoft.com/securityengineering/sdl/threatmodeling.
[5] https://github.com/cairis-platform/cairis.
[6] https://github.com/threatspec/threatspec.

sarial tactics and techniques in MITRE ATLAS. While ThreatFinder.ai internally integrates MITRE ATLAS to inform its threat recommendations, these alignments remain implicit within the tool. Our contribution is to make such links explicit and auditable through knowledge graph transformation and semantic similarity (see Sect. 3.7).

AI-based facial anonymization systems exemplify interdisciplinary security challenges: they must preserve behavioral features (e.g., gaze direction, expressions) while removing identity information for GDPR compliance. Yet recent work shows vulnerabilities to reconstruction and adversarial noise attacks that can recover or leak identity [10,24,25]. These attacks manifest across white-, gray- and black-box settings [19] and are insufficiently mitigated by current defenses, which emphasize classification robustness over anonymization integrity [6,22,23]. This motivates our systematic mapping of threats to mitigations.

Several recent efforts have advanced the state of AI-specific threat modeling. Krone extended ThreatFinder.ai with a large language model (LLM)-powered retrieval-augmented generation (RAG) interface to improve usability and scalability through natural language interaction [27].

Beyond ThreatFinder.ai, other approaches have leveraged structured adversarial taxonomies. For example, studies evaluated MITRE ATLAS's ability to capture AI-specific adversarial behavior [26], while others adapted ATT&CK- and STRIDE-inspired models to address AI pipeline and lifecycle vulnerabilities [8,12]. However, these efforts typically remain either descriptive (taxonomies of attacks and defenses) or tool-specific (extensions of existing security modeling frameworks), and rarely establish explicit machine-readable links between organizational threat assessments and adversarial knowledge bases.

Prior work has either focused on developing ThreatFinder.ai itself or extending it with LLM-based interfaces. In contrast, our contribution explicitly links system-specific outputs from ThreatFinder.ai with adversarial knowledge from MITRE ATLAS, providing an explainable bridge between organizationally usable threat modeling and technically rigorous adversarial taxonomies.

3 Methodology

Methodology Overview. We transform a system-specific threat assessment into a set of semantically linked knowledge graphs that connect organizational risk (assets, threats, controls) with adversarial knowledge (tactics, techniques, mitigations). The approach is designed to meet three concurrent demands: (i) organizational usability and governance auditability, (ii) ethical transparency for privacy-preserving AI, and (iii) technical rigor for adversarial robustness. We demonstrate the method on an AI-based facial anonymization system—an instructive case where GDPR-driven identity removal must coexist with behavioral fidelity and robustness against reconstruction and adversarial noise attacks [10,25]. The methodology proceeds in five phases: (1) system threat modeling in ThreatFinder.ai, (2) construction of a System Threat Modeling Graph (STMG),

(3) construction of reference graphs from the ThreatFinder taxonomy (TFG) and MITRE ATLAS (ATG), (4) cross-graph semantic linking using Sentence-BERT, and (5) validation via structural invariants and interdisciplinary impact checks. Figure 1 shows the system schematic as modeled in ThreatFinder.ai. Each phase reflects technical choices shaped by interdisciplinary design requirements. The details of our semantic linking procedure, including threshold selection and validation, are presented in Sect. 3.7.

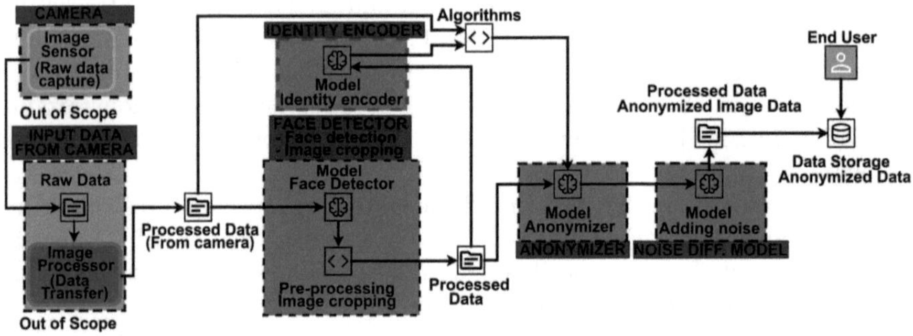

Fig. 1. Schematic representation of the AI system as modeled in ThreatFinder.ai. The diagram includes **12 assets** highlighted in solid black boxes in the figure. These elicited assets served as the basis for selecting threats and assigning mitigating controls, and were later transformed into the STMG for cross-graph reasoning.

3.1 Analyzed System: AI-Based Facial Anonymization Pipeline

The methodology is demonstrated on target-oriented facial anonymization systems, specifically analyzing an AI-based facial anonymization pipeline implementing the Facial Image and Video Anonymization and Anonymization Defense, *FIVA* approach [20]. The system is designed to remove identity information from visual data while preserving behavioral cues such as gaze direction and facial expressions, a critical requirement for maintaining data utility in applications like autonomous driving and human-computer interaction. Unlike traditional anonymization methods that degrade data quality through blurring, pixelation, or masking, this class of systems uses encoder-decoder architectures with identity conditioning to generate realistic anonymized faces while preserving behavioral attributes. *FIVA* employs generative neural networks to synthesize new facial appearances rather than obscuring existing ones, following principles similar to recent frameworks like *FaceDancer* [21] that disentangle identity features from non-identity representations to enable realistic, privacy-preserving face synthesis.

The system's modular architecture (illustrated in Fig. 1) includes components for face detection, identity encoding, anonymization generation, identity tracking, and blending mechanisms. This generative approach maintains data utility for downstream AI tasks (expression recognition, gaze estimation, pose analysis) while ensuring GDPR compliance through identity removal. However, the sophistication of these manipulation-based methods introduces new attack surfaces, including reconstruction attacks where adversarial models attempt to reverse the anonymization, making them ideal candidates for comprehensive threat modeling.

The complete system was modeled in ThreatFinder.ai to systematically identify asset-level threats (e.g., data poisoning, model extraction, adversarial examples) and their corresponding security controls across the AI/ML pipeline. While we demonstrate our methodology on *FIVA*, the approach generalizes to other target-oriented anonymization methods, such as *DeepPrivacy2* [9] and *FALCO* [4], to name a few.

3.2 Initial ThreatFinder.ai Analysis

The initial step in our methodology involved applying the ThreatFinder.ai tool to the AI-based facial anonymization system. The process started with constructing a schematic of the system (see Fig. 1), which ThreatFinder uses as the entry point for analysis. From this schematic, the tool guided us through three core steps: (i) eliciting the system's **assets**, (ii) performing **threat analysis** by selecting relevant threats for each asset, and (iii) performing **control identification** by assigning candidate security controls to mitigate those threats.

In total, the schematic in Fig. 1 included **12 assets**, which served as the foundation for the analysis. Across these assets, the workflow produced **33 threats in total (7 unique)** and **157 security controls (28 unique)**. Importantly, these were instantiated (system-specific) nodes rather than generic taxonomy entries. For example, the asset *Raw Data* was associated with the threat *Data Poisoning*, which was mitigated by controls such as `#DATAQUALITYCONTROL` and `#SEGREGATEDATA`. This yields an auditable reasoning chain: Raw Data(Asset) $\xrightarrow{\texttt{has\_threat}}$ Data Poisoning(Threat) $\xrightarrow{\texttt{mitigated\_by}}$ `#DATAQUALITYCONTROL`(Control). This illustrates how ThreatFinder.ai supports asset-centric modeling by grounding threat modeling in the actual components of a system and linking them to relevant security measures [3].

The value of this step was twofold. First, it grounded our work in a practical tool that has been tested in organizational risk assessments and validated in case studies, ensuring technical rigor and alignment with applied practice. Second, it provided a consistent and structured dataset that we could transform into a graph representation, enabling systematic linking to external reference frameworks such as MITRE ATLAS.

3.3 System Threat Modeling Graph (STMG)

From the ThreatFinder.ai outputs, we constructed what we term the *System Threat Modeling Graph* (STMG). The purpose of the STMG is to capture the system-specific security posture in a knowledge graph structure that can be queried, visualized, and linked to other models.

In the STMG, we represented:

- **Nodes:** Assets, Threats, and Controls.
- **Edges:** Relations between these nodes, specifically:
  - `has_threat`: linking a Threat to the Asset it impacts.
  - `mitigated_by`: linking a Threat to the Control(s) that mitigate it.

The resulting STMG provides a machine-readable and visualizable representation of the AI system's threat landscape. Unlike a tabular threat–control matrix, the STMG preserves relational structure needed for reasoning, deduplication, and cross-framework alignment. It allowed us to go beyond a tabular threat–control list and instead create a relational structure where we can identify, for example, assets facing the highest threat exposure or controls that span multiple threats. This system-specific KG serves as the anchor point for linking with broader taxonomies and reference frameworks.

3.4 KG Schema and Naming Conventions

To enable integration, we normalize entities and relations to a consistent schema shared across the STMG, TFG, and ATG. We use underscores in relation names for consistency.

- **STMG/TFG nodes:** `Asset`, `Threat`, `Control`.
- **ATG nodes:** `Technique`, `SubTechnique`, `Tactic`, `Mitigation`, `CaseStudy`.
- **Relations:**
  - `has_threat` (Asset → Threat), `mitigated_by` (Threat → Control).
  - `affects` (Threat → Asset) in TFG (inverse of `has_threat`).
  - `subtechnique_of` (SubTechnique → Technique), `belongs_to_tactic` (Technique → Tactic), `mitigated_by` (Technique → Mitigation), `describes_technique` (CaseStudy → Technique).
  - `mapped_to`: used for semantic similarity links, i.e., (i) Threat[TFG] → Technique/SubTechnique[ATG], and (ii) Control[TFG/STMG] → Mitigation[ATG].

3.5 ThreatFinder Graph (TFG)

In addition to deriving the STMG from our system-specific analysis, we also constructed a broader graph from the ThreatFinder.ai taxonomy itself. We refer to this graph as the *ThreatFinder Graph* (TFG). While the STMG captures the threats and controls relevant to a single system, the TFG represents the complete threat and control taxonomy provided by the tool.

The TFG was generated from the JSON files available in ThreatFinder.ai, which define generic threats, security controls, and asset categories. In this graph we represented:

- **Nodes:** Generic Threats, Controls, and Assets.
- **Edges:** Relations defined by the taxonomy, specifically:

- applies_to: linking a Control to an Asset category.
- mitigated_by: linking a Threat to the Control(s) that address it.
- affects: linking a Threat to the Asset category it is defined to impact, based on the ThreatFinder ontology (inverse of the STMG relation has_threat).

In total, the TFG defines 49 AI-specific controls, largely derived from the OWASP AI Security & Privacy Guide, which extend across asset categories and can be linked to threats in the taxonomy. These control definitions are curated within ThreatFinder and originate from the OWASP AI Security & Privacy Guide, ensuring alignment with community practice. The purpose of constructing the TFG was to provide a reusable reference layer that extends beyond the context of a single system. By aligning the STMG with the TFG, we established a bridge between system-specific threats and the general threat taxonomy.

3.6 ATLAS Graph (ATG)

We built the *ATLAS Graph* (ATG) from the MITRE ATLAS repository, using the JSON files provided by the project. These files define entities such as adversarial techniques and their relationships, which we transformed into a knowledge graph structure.

In the ATG we represented:

- **Nodes:** Techniques, SubTechniques, Tactics, Mitigations, and Case Studies.
- **Edges:** Relations defined by the ATLAS schema, specifically:
  - belongs_to_tactic: linking a Technique to its associated Tactic.
  - subtechnique_of: linking a SubTechnique to its parent Technique.
  - mitigated_by: linking a Technique to the Mitigation(s) that address it.
  - describes_technique: linking a Case Study to the Technique it exemplifies.

The ATG provides a structured representation of the ATLAS dataset that can be directly linked with our system-specific and taxonomy-based graphs. With STMG, TFG, and ATG in place, we can now link them into a unified multi-layer knowledge graph. The ATG serves as the adversarial reference layer to ground organizational threats in concrete attacker behaviors.

3.7 Linking Across Graphs

After constructing the STMG, TFG, and ATG, we linked them into a unified multi-layer knowledge graph. This step allowed us to connect system-specific threats with the broader ThreatFinder taxonomy and with adversarial techniques described in MITRE ATLAS. Our initial exploration raised the question of whether system-specific threat models produced in ThreatFinder.ai could be meaningfully connected to adversarial knowledge in ATLAS. This motivated the design of our linking strategies, where we combined node reuse with semantic similarity mapping (using SBERT in order to bridge organizational threats with adversarial tactics and techniques.

We applied three complementary strategies for linking:

- **Node reuse:** Threats and controls identified in the STMG were directly aligned with their corresponding nodes in the TFG. This ensured that the system-specific graph was grounded in the broader taxonomy.
- **Semantic similarity mapping:** We embedded the textual descriptions of threats (TFG) and techniques (ATG) using Sentence-BERT (SBERT). For each threat, we identified the most semantically similar techniques and created a `mapped_to` relation, with candidate selection and tie handling following the procedure in Sect. 3 (Semantic Mapping Procedure and Validation). This mapping connects organizational threats to adversarial techniques (TFG → ATG) and, via ATLAS `mitigated_by` relations, situates system-level controls within a broader mitigation landscape. Unlike ThreatFinder's internal rule-based integration, our mapping is explicit and explainable: each link is backed by a similarity score, can be visualized, and can be independently audited.
- **Control-to-mitigation mapping:** In addition to threat→technique mappings, we semantically aligned organizational controls to ATLAS mitigations (Control[TFG/STMG] $\xrightarrow{\texttt{mapped\_to}}$ Mitigation[ATG]) using the same similarity threshold described in the next subsection. This complements ATLAS's intrinsic `mitigated_by` relations from techniques to mitigations.

The result was a unified knowledge graph that spans three levels: the STMG (system-specific), the TFG (taxonomy-based), and the ATG (reference framework). This integration established the foundation for reasoning across technical, organizational, and governance perspectives. This yields auditable, data-driven links (with stored similarity scores) rather than opaque, rule-only associations.

It is important to note that ThreatFinder.ai already integrates MITRE ATLAS internally in its meta-model to support rule-based threat recommendations [2,3]. However, these internal alignments are not exposed for external reasoning and are not semantically grounded. In contrast, our approach transforms ThreatFinder outputs into a dedicated STMG, constructs a full ATG from the MITRE JSON dataset, and performs semantic similarity mapping between TFG threats and ATG techniques. This creates explicit, reproducible, and explainable `mapped_to` relations, enabling cross-graph reasoning that extends beyond ThreatFinder's built-in integration.

3.8 Semantic Mapping Procedure and Validation

We compute semantic similarity between textual descriptions of threats (TFG) and techniques (ATG) using Sentence-BERT (SBERT).

Model Selection: We benchmarked four Sentence-BERT variants on a representative subset of 100 ThreatFinder-ATLAS text pairs to balance semantic accuracy and computational efficiency. Of the tested models, `all-mpnet-base-v2` achieved the highest mean cosine similarity (0.40) and top-1 match score (0.68) but required approximately ten times longer encoding time (1.16 s) than lighter alternatives. `paraphrase-MiniLM-L12-v2` and `all-MiniLM-L6-v2` showed comparable semantic quality (mean similarities 0.36 and 0.35) at substantially lower cost. We selected `all-MiniLM-L6-v2` because it provided the best trade-off between performance and efficiency—yielding stable similarity distributions and interpretable link quality while remaining fast enough (0.12 s per batch) for exhaustive all-pairs comparison across thousands of threat–technique pairs.

Cosine similarity over SBERT embeddings provides candidate links. For each threat t, we retrieve all candidate techniques and retain `mapped_to` edges above a fixed threshold $\tau = 0.60$. We apply the same procedure to controls (TFG/STMG) and mitigations (ATG).

- **Model:** `all-MiniLM-L6-v2` (384-dim) with normalized embeddings.
- **Scoring:** cosine similarity; exhaustive all-pairs search; retain all links above $\tau = 0.60$ (no top-k truncation).
- **Channels:** (i) threat[TFG] $\xrightarrow{\texttt{mapped\_to}}$ technique or SubTechnique [ATG]; (ii) control[TFG/STMG] $\xrightarrow{\texttt{mapped\_to}}$ mitigation [ATG].
- **Disambiguation:** when multiple candidates exceed τ, all are retained; ties are flagged for manual review.

Threshold Selection. We performed a sweep of candidate thresholds ($\tau = 0.50 \ldots 0.75$) and observed the expected trade-off between coverage and precision. At $\tau = 0.50$, many threats and controls were linked but with a large number of weak matches; at $\tau = 0.65+$, coverage dropped sharply. We selected $\tau = 0.60$ as a balanced cutoff. At this threshold, 55 unique threats and 15 unique controls retained at least one mapping, corresponding to 123 threat→technique edges, 72 threat→SubTechnique edges, and 21 control→mitigation edges in total. All similarity scores are preserved as edge attributes, enabling post-hoc filtering or auditing. We also manually spot-checked 20 randomly sampled mappings above τ to verify semantic plausibility.

Sanity Checks. We verified a set of structural invariants to ensure that the unified knowledge graph followed our schema and supported interpretable reasoning:

1. **No direct threat→tactic edges.**
   Threats (from STMG/TFG) must first map to techniques or SubTechniques in ATG through `mapped_to` relations, which then connect to tactics via `belongs_to_tactic`. This guarantees that organizational threat descriptions are grounded in adversarial techniques rather than skipping directly to high-level tactics.
2. **Acyclic SubTechnique hierarchies.**
   All `subtechnique_of` relations form a Directed Acyclic Graph, ensuring that SubTechniques cannot loop back to themselves or create circular definitions, preserving the integrity of the ATLAS taxonomy.

3. **Traceable reasoning chains.**
Every retained `mapped_to` edge appears in at least one valid reasoning path, such as asset → threat → technique/SubTechnique → tactic or threat → control → mitigation. This check prevents the inclusion of dangling or isolated mappings that would break interpretability.

Table 1 summarizes the scale of each layer and the number of semantic links retained by our mapping procedure.

Table 1. Knowledge graph statistics per layer and retained semantic mappings. Node-type breakdowns show the scale of each layer. For semantic mappings (bottom rows), we report both total edge counts (e.g., 123 threat→technique edges) and coverage in terms of unique nodes with at least one mapping. At $\tau = 0.60$, this corresponds to 55 unique threats and 15 unique controls that retained links, yielding 123 threat→technique, 72 threat→SubTechnique, and 21 control→mitigation edges in total.

Layer	#Nodes (#Edges)	Node-type breakdown
STMG	203 (202)	Assets=12, Threats=33, Controls=157, Model=1
TFG	240 (6075)	Assets=74, Threats=117, Controls=49
ATG	188 (448)	Tactics=15, Techniques=68, SubTechniques=47, Mitigations=26, CaseStudies=32
Semantic mappings (retained above $\tau = 0.60$)		
Threat → Technique (`mapped_to`)	123	
Threat → SubTechnique (`mapped_to`)	72	
Control → Mitigation (`mapped_to`)	21	

3.9 Visualization and Reasoning

Once the unified knowledge graph was constructed, we developed interpretive views of its structure to support reasoning over the relations. We highlight three complementary perspectives, all of which can be derived from the same KG representations:

- **Asset-centric views:** focusing on a single asset together with its associated threats, controls, and (where available) mapped adversarial elements. Figure 2, for example, shows the *Identity encoder* asset with five linked threats, their selected controls, and the mapped ATLAS techniques, sub-techniques, tactics, and mitigations.
- **Flowchart views:** interpreting the KG in a layered manner (assets → threats → controls/techniques → tactics), highlighting how threats propagate across levels. This perspective is implicit in Fig. 2, where nodes are arranged to emphasize vertical integration from system-specific threats to adversarial tactics.
- **Chain views:** tracing specific reasoning paths across the KG, such as
$$\text{Asset} \rightarrow \text{Threat} \xrightarrow{\texttt{mapped\_to}} \text{Technique} \xrightarrow{\texttt{belongs\_to\_tactic}} \text{Tactic},$$
making explicit how organizational threats correspond to adversarial behaviors. Such reasoning chains are illustrated in Table 2 (Raw Data → Data Poisoning) and Fig. 2 (Identity Encoder).

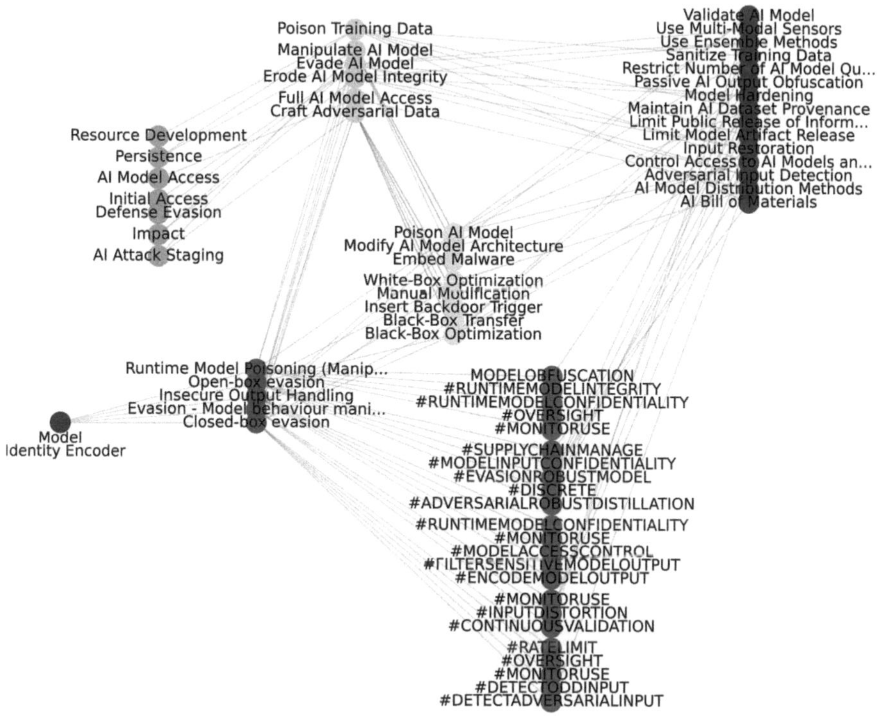

Fig. 2. Asset-centric visualization for the *Identity encoder*. Whereas Table 2 contrasts a simple case (*Raw Data* → *Data Poisoning*), this figure illustrates a more complex asset. The *Identity encoder* is linked to five threats (green), their selected organizational controls (red), and mapped ATLAS techniques and sub-techniques (yellow/khaki), tactics (orange), and mitigations (brown). The figure highlights how the unified KG captures broader threat surfaces and shows where vulnerabilities cluster or controls overlap.

Together, these perspectives show how the unified KG can be read at different levels: asset-centric views reveal an individual component's posture, flowchart views emphasize how threats propagate across layers, and chain views provide explicit reasoning traces for auditability. This flexibility demonstrates how a single KG structure can support organizational, technical, and governance needs simultaneously. Figure 2 extends the comparison in Table 2 by showing how a more complex asset can be represented in full context, enabling reasoning across organizational and adversarial layers.

Implementation Note. The pipeline was implemented in Python using standard libraries: NetworkX for graph construction, Pandas for preprocessing JSON and tabular data, Sentence-BERT (SBERT) for semantic similarity mapping, and Matplotlib for visualization. The workflow was modular—parsing JSONs, constructing STMG/TFG/ATG, performing semantic linking, and exporting visualizations— with stable identifiers preserved to ensure traceability and reproducibility. We used NetworkX 3.x, Pandas 2.x, and sentence-transformers 2.x (model `all-MiniLM-L6-v2`). Random seeds were fixed for reproducibility. All graphs (STMG, TFG, ATG) and cross-graph `mapped_to` edges were exported as JSON/CSV with stable identifiers.

4 Results and Demonstration

4.1 Graph Statistics and Coverage

The unified knowledge graph combines the STMG, TFG, and ATG into a single structure. Table 1 reports node and edge counts across layers, including the number of semantic `mapped_to` relations created during linking. Overall, 117 threats and 49 controls were available in the ThreatFinder taxonomy. Of these, 55 threats (47%) mapped to at least one ATLAS technique or SubTechnique, while 15 controls (31%) mapped to ATLAS mitigations.

These coverage rates reveal the actionable overlap between organizational and adversarial security perspectives. ThreatFinder includes governance- and process-oriented threats (e.g., compliance failures, policy gaps) that have no direct adversarial technique counterparts, while ATLAS documents technical attack behaviors (e.g., specific evasion methods) that may not align with organizational threat taxonomies. The 47% threat mapping identifies precisely those organizational concerns that correspond to documented adversarial behaviors, enabling practitioners to connect their asset-centric assessments to concrete attack techniques. Similarly, the 31% control-to-mitigation alignment reveals which organizational controls directly address adversarially-validated mitigations. A full overlap would indicate redundancy between frameworks; instead, this complementarity demonstrates that each perspective contributes distinct security value, while our approach bridges their intersection for cross-layer reasoning.

4.2 Example Reasoning Chains

To illustrate how the unified KG supports reasoning, we first focus on the threat *Data Poisoning* as it appears for the *Raw Data* asset. In the STMG, this asset is linked to one threat and four selected controls. The TFG shows the taxonomy-level view with all 49 controls available in ThreatFinder.ai, illustrating the broader design space. The Unified KG then enriches the same threat with adversarial mappings from MITRE ATLAS, linking to techniques, tactics, and mitigations. Table 2 summarizes these three perspectives, showing how our methodology narrows generic taxonomies to system-relevant measures and connects them to adversarial knowledge.

While this example highlights a relatively simple case, other assets in the system show more complex threat surfaces. Figure 2 illustrates this by visualizing the *Identity Encoder* asset, which is connected to five threats, their mitigating controls, and the corresponding adversarial mappings. Together, the table and figure demonstrate how the unified KG supports reasoning across assets of varying complexity, enabling analysts to trace both minimal and broader attack surfaces within the same system.

Table 2. Perspectives on the threat *Data Poisoning* for the *Raw Data* asset. The table contrasts three KG views: the system-specific STMG with four selected controls, the taxonomy-level TFG with all 49 available controls, and the Unified KG enriched with adversarial mappings from MITRE ATLAS. This simple case provides a baseline for comparison with more complex assets such as the *Identity Encoder* in Fig. 2.

View	Asset → Threat	Controls	Adversarial links
STMG (system-specific)	Raw Data → Data Poisoning	4 selected: #SEGREGATEDATA, #DEVDATAPROTECT, #DATAQUALITYCONTROL, #DATAMINIMIZE	—
TFG (taxonomy)	Raw Data → Data Poisoning	49 available ThreatFinder.ai controls	—
Unified KG	Raw Data → Data Poisoning	4 selected (same as STMG)	Technique: *Poison Training Data* → Tactics: *Persistence, Resource Development*; → Mitigations: *Sanitize Training Data, Maintain AI Dataset Provenance, Limit Model Artifact Release, Control Access to AI Models, AI Bill of Materials*

4.3 Cross-Layer Reasoning

The unified KG supports cross-layer reasoning that bridges technical threats, mitigations, and organizational implications. For example, organizational threats such as *Model Extraction* can be traced through their mapped ATLAS techniques (e.g., *Model Stealing*) to corresponding tactics (*Exfiltration*), and further linked to mitigating controls and organizational safeguards. This enables analysts to not only identify technical vulnerabilities but also evaluate how these connect to higher-level governance structures, aligning with the responsible AI perspective discussed in Sect. 2.

5 Conclusion

We have shown that semantic knowledge graph integration can bridge organizational threat modeling with adversarial frameworks for AI security assessment. Applied to a facial anonymization system, ThreatFinder.ai identified 12 assets, 33 instantiated threats (7 unique), and 157 instantiated controls (28 unique). By transforming these outputs into explicit knowledge graphs (STMG) and semantically linking them with the ThreatFinder taxonomy (TFG) and MITRE ATLAS (ATG) using SBERT, we established 123 threat→technique,

72 threat→subTechnique, and 21 control→mitigation alignments, covering 55 unique threats and 15 unique controls. These results demonstrate that organizationally defined threats can meaningfully align with adversarial knowledge bases.

While this work establishes technical feasibility, validation with security practitioners is a critical next step. Anticipated benefits include reduced cognitive load through asset-centric views, transparent audit trails connecting controls to adversarial mitigations, and explicit gap identification where threats or controls lack coverage. Controlled studies could assess analyst performance using our unified KG versus baseline tools.

The methodology generalizes beyond facial anonymization: any AI/ML system modeled in ThreatFinder.ai can be transformed and linked to ATLAS, enabling repeatable workflows in domains such as healthcare, finance, and autonomous driving.

While the chosen SBERT variant (`all-MiniLM-L6-v2`) achieved an effective balance between semantic precision and computational efficiency, future work could explore domain-adapted or fine-tuned embedding models specifically trained on AI-security corpora to further improve terminological alignment between organizational threats and adversarial techniques.

Future integration of retrieval-augmented generation (RAG) could enhance usability, while semantic linking provides explicit, auditable bridges between organizational and adversarial perspectives—a foundation for advancing automated reasoning and standardized evaluation practices in AI security.

Acknowledgment. This research was funded by the Swedish innovation agency Vinnova under the project *Anonymization Defense GUARD (GUarding Anonymization pRoceDures)* (reference number: 2023-02996). This work was also supported in part by the European Union's Horizon Europe research and innovation programme through the project *ATHENA – An exposition on THe forEign informatioN mAnipulation and interference* (Grant Agreement 101132686 ATHENA HORIZON-CL2-2023-DEMOCRACY-01). The authors are also grateful to Martin Torstensson for setting up the GUARD project and to Dr. Felix Rosberg for providing access to the facial anonymization models.

Disclosure of Interests. The authors have no competing interests to declare that are relevant to the content of this article.

References

1. Al-Sada, B., Sadighian, A., Oligeri, G.: Mitre att&ck: State of the art and way forward. ACM Comput. Surv. **57**(1) (2024). https://doi.org/10.1145/3687300
2. Von der Assen, J., Huertas, A., Sharif, J., Feng, C., Bovet, G., Stiller, B.: Threatfinderai: automated threat modeling applied to LLM system integration. In: 2024 20th International Conference on Network and Service Management (CNSM), pp. 1–3 (2024). https://doi.org/10.23919/CNSM62983.2024.10814632

3. Von der Assen, J., Sharif, J., Feng, C., Killer, C., Bovet, G., Stiller, B.: Asset-centric threat modeling for ai-based systems. In: 2024 IEEE International Conference on Cyber Security and Resilience (CSR), pp. 437–444 (2024). https://doi.org/10.1109/CSR61664.2024.10679445
4. Barattin, S., Tzelepis, C., Patras, I., Sebe, N.: Attribute-preserving face dataset anonymization via latent code optimization. In: Proceedings of the IEEE/CVF Conference on Computer Vision and Pattern Recognition, pp. 8001–8010 (2023)
5. European Union Agency for Cybersecurity (ENISA): Enisa threat landscape 2024. Technical Report, ENISA (2024). https://www.enisa.europa.eu/publications/enisa-threat-landscape-2024. European Union Agency for Cybersecurity
6. Goodfellow, I.J., Shlens, J., Szegedy, C.: Explaining and harnessing adversarial examples. arXiv preprint arXiv:1412.6572 (2014)
7. Habbal, A., Ali, M.K., Abuzaraida, M.A.: Artificial intelligence trust, risk and security management (AI TRISM): frameworks, applications, challenges and future research directions. Expert Syst. Appl. **240**, 122442 (2024)
8. Hu, Y., et al.: Artificial intelligence security: Threats and countermeasures. ACM Comput. Surv. **55**(1) (2021). https://doi.org/10.1145/3487890
9. Hukkelås, H., Lindseth, F.: Deepprivacy2: Towards realistic full-body anonymization. In: Proceedings of the IEEE/CVF winter Conference on Applications of Computer Vision, pp. 1329–1338 (2023)
10. Hussain, S., et al.: Reface: Real-time adversarial attacks on face recognition systems. arXiv preprint arXiv:2206.04783 (2022)
11. Jedrzejewski, F.V., Thode, L., Fischbach, J., Gorschek, T., Mendez, D., Lavesson, N.: Adversarial machine learning in industry: a systematic literature review. Comput. Secur. **145**, 103988 (2024)
12. Mauri, L., Damiani, E.: Modeling threats to ai-ml systems using stride. Sensors **22** (2022). https://doi.org/10.3390/s22176662
13. Miller, G.A.: The magical number seven, plus or minus two: some limits on our capacity for processing information. Psychol. Rev. **63**(2), 81 (1956)
14. Mink, J., Kaur, H., Schmüser, J., Fahl, S., Acar, Y.: {Security} is not my field,{I'm} a stats {guy}: a qualitative root cause analysis of barriers to adversarial machine learning defenses in industry. In: 32nd USENIX Security Symposium (USENIX Security 23), pp. 3763–3780 (2023)
15. MITRE Corporation: Mitre atlas (adversarial threat landscape for artificial-intelligence systems) (2023). https://atlas.mitre.org/. global, living knowledge base of AI adversarial tactics and techniques
16. Neupane, S., et al.: Security considerations in ai-robotics: A survey of current methods, challenges, and opportunities. IEEE Access **12**, 22072–22097 (2024). https://doi.org/10.1109/ACCESS.2024.3363657
17. OWASP AI Exchange Project: Owasp ai security & privacy guide (2021). https://owasp.org/www-project-ai-security-and-privacy-guide/. working online guide
18. Reimers, N., Gurevych, I.: Sentence-BERT: Sentence embeddings using Siamese BERT-networks (2019). https://arxiv.org/abs/1908.10084
19. Ren, K., Zheng, T., Qin, Z., Liu, X.: Adversarial attacks and defenses in deep learning. Engineering **6**(3), 346–360 (2020)
20. Rosberg, F., Aksoy, E.E., Englund, C., Alonso-Fernandez, F.: Fiva: facial image and video anonymization and anonymization defense. In: Proceedings of the IEEE/CVF International Conference on Computer Vision, pp. 362–371 (2023)
21. Rosberg, F.: FaceDancer: Facial Identity Manipulation for Privacy-Preserving Computer Vision. Ph.D. thesis, Chalmers University of Technology, Gothen-

burg, Sweden (2023). https://www.diva-portal.org/smash/get/diva2:1845212/FULLTEXT01.pdf
22. Samangouei, P., Kabkab, M., Chellappa, R.: Defense-GAN: Protecting classifiers against adversarial attacks using generative models. arXiv preprint arXiv:1805.06605 (2018)
23. Stock, P., Shilov, I., Mironov, I., Sablayrolles, A.: Defending against reconstruction attacks with rényi differential privacy. arXiv preprint arXiv:2202.07623 (2022)
24. Vakhshiteh, F., Nickabadi, A., Ramachandra, R.: Adversarial attacks against face recognition: a comprehensive study. IEEE Access **9**, 92735–92756 (2021)
25. Wang, Z., Song, M., Zhang, Z., Song, Y., Wang, Q., Qi, H.: Beyond inferring class representatives: User-level privacy leakage from federated learning. In: IEEE INFOCOM 2019-IEEE Conference on Computer Communications, pp. 2512–2520. IEEE (2019)
26. Wymberry, C., Jahankhani, H.: An approach to measure the effectiveness of the mitre atlas framework in safeguarding machine learning systems against data poisoning attack. In: Cybersecurity and artificial intelligence: transformational strategies and disruptive innovation, pp. 81–116. Springer (2024)
27. Wäspi, R.: Design and evaluation of a large language model-powered threat modeling approach with applications to ai security (2025)

Towards Trustworthy AI: A Framework for Integrating Ethics Committees into Product Development

Lilit Wecker[1(✉)], Jeppe Agger Nielsen[1], Kamal Nasrollahi[2], and Thomas Ploug[3,4]

[1] Aalborg University, Aalborg, Denmark
lwec@create.aau.dk
[2] Aalborg University, Milestone Systems A/S, Aalborg, Denmark
[3] Aalborg University, Copenhagen, Denmark
[4] Halmstad University, Halmstad, Sweden

Abstract. Product teams developing artificial intelligence (AI) increasingly create solutions with societal consequences and ethical implications. However, they often lack the ability to anticipate or mitigate ethical risks during development, relying primarily on legal compliance review and ex-post accountability. To address this challenge, this paper proposes that product teams can learn from structured ethical oversight procedures, well-established in healthcare, defense, and other high-stakes domains. Guided by this logic, we introduce the Sprint Ethics Board (SEB), a lightweight governance framework that adapts established committee models to agile workflows in product teams. The SEB is defined by three features (1) clear trigger points tied to product milestones, (2) a core group of members—product decision authority, ethical and domain expertise, and an external stakeholder advocate—that together form the minimum credible quorum for oversight, and (3) artefacts—a one-page Ethics Brief and a machine-readable Decision Log—that integrate into the sprint toolchain in product development. Together, these features enable the SEB to satisfy regulatory demand and move toward trustworthy AI in product development. The paper offers a design framework and outlines a research agenda to evaluate the SEB empirically in industry contexts. By suggesting how ethical review procedures can be translated into agile decision-making in product teams, the SEB reframes ethics oversight from a retrospective safeguard into a proactive, enforceable, and auditable function of product delivery. If adopted, the SEB framework can serve as a firm foundation for Ethical AI development.

Keywords: Product Development · Ethics Committee · AI Governance · Trustworthy AI

1 Introduction

A product team at a video analytics firm is hours away from shipping a new face-recognition feature. The latest build shows measurable performance gains—yet a single threshold change could suddenly flag thousands more people for review. Who should

K. Nasrollahi et al. (Eds.): REPAI-W 2025, LNCS 16390, pp. 41–56, 2026.
https://doi.org/10.1007/978-3-032-16886-3_3

decide whether that risk is acceptable? In many AI-driven product teams, the answer remains narrow: the product manager (and their line manager), supplemented by a hurried legal check. Such practices leave consequential ethical trade-offs without structured deliberation or accountable decision rights [1].

By contrast, regulated domains such as healthcare, dual-use research, and medical-device development operate with Ethics Committees (ECs). Clinical Ethics Committees convene multidisciplinary expertise, maintain auditable records, and in many cases possess authority to halt or modify projects when harms outweigh benefits [2, 3]. In the security domain, so-called "dual-use" technologies—those with both civilian and military applications, such as advanced cryptography or facial recognition—are subject to oversight bodies that evaluate export risks and national-security implications [4]. Their procedures integrate ethical reflection into decision-making in ways that commercial product teams in the context of AI development rarely match. Technology firms have experimented with ethics oversight, but results are uneven. Google's Advanced Technology External Advisory Council dissolved within a week, its legitimacy undermined by disputes over remit and member selection [5, 6]. Microsoft has taken the opposite path, introducing a Responsible AI Council that reviews systems at every product milestone, while Salesforce's Office of Ethical & Humane Use includes external advocates in roadmap discussions. Yet, public evidence suggests limited decision power for either board: most corporate AI ethics bodies remain advisory, lack formal veto rights, and are only weakly coupled to day-to-day product governance [7–9]. The Sprint Ethics Board is proposed precisely to counter these weaknesses by embedding decision authority in a sprint-level quorum, coupling ethical deliberation to release gates, and making veto decisions traceable through lightweight artefacts integrated into the development toolchain.

In response, scholars have distilled design principles for corporate AI ethics boards—including independence, diversity, stakeholder input, decision logs, and real veto authority—that industry practice has only partially adopted [9]. Agile product-development teams further complicate the picture. Delivering in one- or two-week sprints, they privilege speed and iteration. As a result, ethical deliberation is often relegated to post-hoc compliance checks, if it happens at all. A recent systematic review of "ethics-aware" software-engineering practices found that most tools target individual developer conduct, rather than organizational decision rights [10]. Moreover, ethnographic studies of AI-enabled health projects show how agile teams default to siloed compliance and lack forums for cross-functional risk arbitration [11]. Structural asymmetries persist: the authority to delay or block release decisions typically lies only with legal/compliance teams—or with no one at all [12]. This leaves product managers accountable for choices they cannot unilaterally stop, and legal staff tasked with interpreting societal values they were not hired to govern [13, 14].

This paper advances a position: product teams should not invent ethical governance principles from scratch but adapt lessons from established ethical committee models into agile-compatible forms. We propose the *Sprint Ethics Board (SEB)* as a lightweight governance framework tailored to contemporary product management teams. Inspired by the practices of Clinical Ethics Committees, Institutional Review Boards, and regulatory audit bodies, the SEB integrates three core features: (1) structured deliberation triggered at key points in product cycles (from strategic roadmaps to release increments); (2) a minimum credible quorum combining product authority, ethical expertise, and stakeholder voice; and (3) two lightweight artefacts—a one-page Ethics Brief and a Decision Log—that preserve traceability without undermining delivery velocity. Building on institutional translation theory [15, 16]; the SEB can be understood as a *translation mechanism*—a bridge between high-level ethical theorization (e.g., principles, standards, and regulatory frameworks) and localized agile practices. Rather than claiming empirical validation, this paper's contribution is *conceptual*: it formulates SEB as a design proposal that can be empirically examined in future work through, for instance, a single-case study of responsible AI implementation in specific organizational contexts. This approach aligns with the Scandinavian institutionalist view that ideas travel and transform through translation, repurposing, and localized enactment [17, 18]. In doing so, SEBs aim to bridge the persistent principle–practice gap that separates responsible AI frameworks from product reality. As Jobin et al. [19] show in their global survey, the proliferation of AI ethics guidelines has outpaced mechanisms for operationalization. SEB responds to this imbalance by embedding ethical deliberation into existing agile structures, enabling organizations to translate normative aspirations into accountable, auditable decisions. Rather than prescribing a single implementation, this paper positions SEB as a design framework—a foundation for experimentation and adaptation across diverse organizational contexts.

2 Ethics Committees

Ethical decision-making in high-stakes domains has long relied on ethics committees. Clinical Ethics Committees (CECs) and Institutional Review Boards (IRBs) represent well-established models in healthcare and research. They perform three critical functions: (1) convening multidisciplinary expertise to deliberate on ethically charged decisions; (2) maintaining transparent, auditable records; and (3) holding authority to pause or redirect projects when risks outweigh anticipated benefits [2, 3, 20]. In dual-use research and defense innovation, analogous oversight bodies exist to scrutinize technologies with potential for unintended societal or security harms [4]. Scholars have distilled a set of design principles for effective ethics boards: independence from product sponsors, diversity of expertise, stakeholder participation, clear decision logs, sunset clauses to prevent capture, and genuine veto authority [9]. These principles offer a conceptual baseline, yet adoption in the technology sector remains partial and uneven. For agile product-development teams, the gap is especially stark. While committees in healthcare or defense are designed to deliberate at weeks- or months-long intervals, agile organizations typically operate on one- to two-week sprint cycles, where most decisions are made under intense time pressure. This tempo leaves little room for traditional review procedures, meaning that by the time a release is "hours away," as in the opening example, ethical reflection often comes too late to meaningfully influence outcomes. The Sprint Ethics Board (SEB) does not aim to intervene at the final release moment but to shift deliberation earlier—embedding lightweight checkpoints throughout the sprint cycle so that potential risks surface when design choices are still reversible and mitigations still feasible. Governance mechanisms that rely on lengthy review procedures are therefore seen as incompatible with delivery velocity. As a result, ethical considerations are often displaced into retrospective audits, advisory checklists, or compliance silos—none of which answer the fundamental governance question of *who holds authority to stop a release.* In most software organizations, that authority informally resides with the *product leadership function* (e.g., product director or head of product), which balances delivery and risk. The Sprint Ethics Board (SEB) formalizes this structure: it grants product leadership explicit veto rights when consensus cannot be reached, while ensuring that ethical, legal, and stakeholder perspectives are represented in deliberation. This creates an accountable decision locus that mirrors the authority logic of CECs without replicating their bureaucratic overhead. From a theoretical standpoint, this adaptation can be read through the lens of *translation theory* [15, 21]. Ethics committees, as institutional templates, are *translated* into a new organizational setting—agile software development—where their purpose, cadence, and artifacts must be re-edited to achieve contextual legitimacy. Rather than copying existing governance forms ("faithful imitation"), SEB exemplifies *repurposing* and *localized translation* [17, 18]: it retains core principles of transparency and authority but re-materializes them in agile routines such as sprint planning and release gating. This structural mismatch between traditional committees and agile workflows therefore points not to rejection but to *reinterpretation.* SEB is proposed as precisely such an adaptation—lightweight, cadence-matched, and explicitly oriented toward redistributing decision rights in contexts where speed is prized but legitimacy is underdeveloped. Future empirical work will examine how SEB's translation unfolds in practice—whether teams replicate, modify, or resist its governance logic—contributing to a broader understanding of how ethical oversight mechanisms travel across institutional domains.

2.1 Comparing Four Archetypes

Ethics oversight is not a monolith. Clinical practice, academic research, dual-use export control, and medical-device regulation have each evolved a distinctive commit-tee type—yet all four confront the same basic question: who has the authority, process, and evidence to determine not only *whether* a project should stop, but *how* and *when* ethical risks must be addressed? To assess which elements can be translated into sprint-based product development, we benchmark these archetypes in Table 1, along four dimensions—trigger, membership, mandate, and agility pain-points—then distil features that inform the Sprint Ethics Board (SEB).

Common features: Despite differences in tempo, all four archetypes share three structural traits. *First,* multidisciplinary membership: CECs convene clinical and ethical voices, IRBs mix scientific and lay perspectives, and dual-use boards combine technical and security expertise. *Second,* documented deliberation: each committee issues an artefact—consultation report, approval letter, dossier, or certificate—that records rationale and conditions, satisfying regulators' demands for traceability [10–13]. *Third,* decision authority: IRBs, dual-use boards, and Notified Bodies have explicit veto rights, while CEC recommendations strongly influence immediate clinical action. Embedding a comparable decision lever—scaled to agile timeframes—into sprint governance is therefore both feasible and desirable.

Table 1. Ethics committee archetypes: trigger points, membership composition, and agility pain-points.

Archetype	Trigger	Membership	Pain-points
Clinical Ethics Committee	Request from ward when a patient-care dilemma surfaces (often < 24 h turnaround)	Physicians, nurses, clinical ethicist, occasionally legal counsel & chaplain	Time pressure; advisory only—implementation can lag [3]
Institutional Review Board	Submission of research protocol before any human-subject interaction; annual continuing review	Scientists, non-scientists, independent community member	Heavy paperwork; meetings 30–45 days apart [20]
Security/Dual-use Committee	License application or prototype export request	Government export-control officials, defense technologists, security lawyers	Secrecy slows peer input; veto may conflict with business deadlines [4]
Notified Body for SaMD	Conformity-assessment audit before first market release and at each "significant change" (e.g., new algorithm)	Third-party auditors with software, clinical and QMS expertise	Audit cycle takes weeks; every major software update triggers re-review [22]

Translation and transfer hurdles: However, direct import of these committee models into agile product teams introduces three recurring frictions—latency, confidentiality, and cost. *First,* timelines: ethics reviews in healthcare or research may take weeks or months, whereas agile teams release features in days. *Second,* confidentiality: dual-use technologies are often reviewed under strict secrecy, but product teams rely on open collaboration and fast feedback, which secrecy undermines. *Third*, cost: regulatory audits in medical devices can require tens of thousands of euros and weeks of review—an investment most software teams cannot sustain for each release [22, 23]. From a translation-theory perspective [15, 21], these frictions illustrate what happens when institutional templates travel across fields: meanings, tempos, and artefacts must be re-edited to maintain legitimacy. Agile teams cannot copy existing committees; they must translate them. The SEB therefore represents a localized translation—repurposing the deliberative logic of ethics committees within the cadence and decision rights of sprint management [17, 18]. In organizations practicing continuous integration and continuous deployment (CI/CD), the same logic can extend beyond discrete sprints: SEB checkpoints may evolve into rolling, lightweight reviews synchronized with release pipelines. This shift would make ethical oversight itself a continuous process—tested iteratively, much like the code it governs—and represents an important direction for empirical evaluation.

To make oversight viable for sprint teams, the SEB redesigns core traits through tiered reviews, scoped NDAs, and lightweight artefacts—faithful enough to preserve legitimacy, yet adaptive enough to sustain delivery speed. In this sense, SEB functions as a repurposed hybrid: an institutional idea that travels from healthcare and defense into software practice, gaining new form while retaining its ethical intent.

2.2 From Archetypes to Agile Checkpoints

Agile teams in product development operate at tempos unfamiliar to regulators accustomed to monthly or yearly cycles. Yet the four archetypes of ethics oversight already embody *decision moments* that, when *translated* into the agile domain, align with sprint milestones. This translation process does not reproduce formal procedures but *repurposes* their underlying logic—embedding ethical deliberation at moments where teams already pause for reflection. Translating these triggers into agile language reveals where structured ethical dialogue can occur without derailing delivery flow. *(1) Backlog grooming/refinement – IRB pre-protocol review.* Early triage of backlog items mirrors IRB practices, where foreseeable risks are flagged before research begins. In agile teams, this checkpoint surfaces ethically sensitive features while they are still conceptual, avoiding wasted engineering effort and enabling proportionate mitigations [20]. *(2) Sprint planning and design reviews – CEC bedside consultations.* Like Clinical Ethics Committees convened under time pressure, SEBs can host short, multidisciplinary deliberations during sprint planning. Most cases resolve quickly; more complex dilemmas can extend into structured discussions within the sprint [3]. (3) *Pre-release checkpoints – Notified Body conformity audits.* These represent binary release decisions. SEBs adapt this through a tiered review model: routine features receive lightweight checks, while high-risk features trigger expanded, multi-session deliberations before deployment [22]. (4) *Post-release monitoring – IRB continuing review & SaMD audits.* Significant changes—such as altered data sources, adjusted thresholds, or newly observed harms—re-trigger SEB review. This ongoing monitoring aligns with the "continuing review" duty of IRBs and post-market audits for medical software, embedding ethical vigilance across the lifecycle [20, 22]. Crucially, the SEB's role is not to *halt* agile practices but to enable dynamic decision-support. Low-risk features move quickly, while high-risk features receive the additional time, expertise, and collaborative problem-solving they require. By embedding these four checkpoints—concept, design, release, and post-release—into the sprint rhythm, SEBs evolve from bolt-on compliance gates into integrated governance mechanisms that keep pace with continuous delivery. From a translation-theory perspective [15, 24], this reconfiguration exemplifies *high-mode translation*: abstract ethical oversight principles are re-encoded into operational routines. The SEB thus converts institutional logics of caution, deliberation, and traceability into agile artefacts that are fast, iterative, and participatory. This transformation illustrates how ideas *travel* and acquire legitimacy through contextual adaptation rather than literal reproduction [17, 18].

2.3 The Role of Ethics Committees Across the Agile Product Development Lifecycle

While the mapping in Sect. 2.2 identified structural parallels, it remains schematic. To make the argument more concrete, the following discussion illustrates how these oversight "moments" align with the sprint lifecycle—concept, design, release, and post-deployment—showing that ethical deliberation can be integrated into existing checkpoints without disrupting delivery flow. At the *concept stage*, backlog grooming parallels IRB pre-protocol reviews, flagging foreseeable risks before engineering begins [20]. During *design*, sprint planning resembles bedside consultations in Clinical Ethics Committees, enabling concise, multidisciplinary dialogue for routine dilemmas [3]. The *release stage* echoes Notified-Body conformity audits, introducing a binary gate - release or delay - through tiered reviews [22]. Finally, *post-deployment* monitoring mirrors IRB continuing review and regulatory audits, ensuring that ethical reflection remains continuous [20, 22]. Seen from a translation theory perspective [16, 25], these checkpoints demonstrate how institutional templates can be localized through modification and adaptation. Some SEBs might reproduce committee logic "faithfully," while others will alter or streamline it to fit team culture [17]. Such variation is expected, turning SEB into an *experimental translation* of ethical governance rather than a static compliance tool. Future empirical work is encouraged to trace these translations in situ—observing how ethical reasoning travels through sprint artefacts, meetings, and release gates over time.

3 A Framework for the Sprint Ethics Board

The Sprint Ethics Board (SEB) constitutes the practical translation of established ethics-committee principles into the tempo, artefacts, and authority structures of agile product development. In theoretical terms, SEB functions as a translation device [15, 16] that carries normative logics from one context (clinical and regulatory ethics) into another (software engineering/product development), where they must be re-contextualized to become legitimate and workable [15, 26]. The framework that follows describes how this translation occurs through its trigger points, membership composition, and artefacts.

3.1 Trigger Points

Ethics committees can only influence outcomes when their deliberations align with the tempo of decision-making in a domain. For agile and AI-driven product development, this means synchronizing oversight with sprint checkpoints rather than introducing external gates that slow delivery. The SEB adapts key functions from clinical, research, and regulatory committees to the agile cadence, integrating ethical reviews where they most directly shape outcomes. Three primary trigger points anchor its operation: (1) *Concept stage***.** During backlog grooming and early refinement, stories remain conceptual. A brief triage here identifies foreseeable risks and flags ethically sensitive features before heavy engineering begins. This is the lowest-cost intervention point, analogous to IRB pre-protocol review [20]. *(2) Pre-release stage.* Before deployment, the SEB provides a binary decision: proceed or delay until mitigations are in place. To balance speed with diligence, the model uses tiered reviews: routine features undergo lightweight checks, while high-risk items may escalate into deeper, multi-session deliberation within the same sprint [22]. *(3) Post-deployment stage.* Ethical oversight does not end at release. Like continuing IRB review or regulatory "significant change" audits, the SEB reconvenes whenever inputs, thresholds, or observed harms shift. This enables iterative mitigation and rollback decisions, ensuring that oversight is continuous rather than front-loaded

[20, 22]. By aligning its scope with these three trigger points, the SEB embeds ethical reflection in the sprint rhythm. Rather than being an external hurdle, it becomes a translation layer that converts abstract governance obligations into sprint-compatible decision routines [17, 18].

3.2 Membership and Roles

The effectiveness of any ethics committee depends on its composition. All four archetypes reviewed earlier demonstrate that multidisciplinarity is non-negotiable: CECs blend clinicians and ethicists, IRBs balance scientists with community voices, and Notified Bodies combine technical and regulatory expertise [3, 20, 22]. The SEB extends this logic into agile product teams, while adapting membership to the realities of sprint cadence.

Agile team theory and practice emphasize maintaining small, cross-functional groups—typically under ten members—to preserve focus, communication clarity, and self-organization [27, 28]. Including peripheral roles—such as legal or compliance officers—in every sprint event would increase cognitive load and conflict with timeboxing principles. Instead, SEBs rely on a *core quorum* (product manager, engineer, designer, ethicist, and external advocate) to flag potential ethical risks early, invoking *adjunct expertise* only when warranted by the feature's sensitivity or scope. This preserves sprint agility while enabling structured escalation [29, 30].

Suggested core members (standing):

- *Product manager* – anchors deliberations in backlog priorities and delivery constraints [10].
- *Software engineer/data scientist* – translates proposed mitigations into feasible technical options.
- *Designer* – ensures user-experience impacts and potential usability harms are *surfaced.*
- Ethics or responsible innovation lead – provides normative framing, drawing on frameworks such as IEEE 7000 or ISO/IEC 42001 [13, 14]
- *Independent lay or domain representative* – mirrors the IRB model, bringing an external, user-centric perspective that counters organizational blind spots [7].

Suggested adjunct members (rotating):

Depending on feature scope, the SEB can invite temporary members such as:

- Legal/compliance officer – for issues tied to regulation, such as EU AI Act obligations [31].
- Security or dual-use expert – when export-control or national-security implications arise [4].
- UX researcher or clinician – where usability and safety risks overlap, particularly in health-related applications [11].

Suggested roles and responsibilities:

- The chair rotates, preventing capture by a single discipline and encouraging balanced deliberation [8].

- The scribe maintains a one-page ethics brief and machine-readable decision log, ensuring traceability without imposing the paperwork burdens typical of IRBs or regulatory audits [10].
- All members share responsibility for articulating concerns and weighing mitigations, with escalation rules ensuring that unresolved disagreements are flagged at the organizational level.

Empirical work shows that external perspectives often surface justice concerns overlooked by developers [32], reinforcing the inclusion of a lay member. This hybrid membership model mirrors agile's logic: a stable core supplemented by just-in-time expertise. In translation-theory terms, SEB membership embodies actor hybridization—a deliberate recombination of professional roles that re-materializes ethical deliberation within sprint teams [33, 34].

3.3 Artefacts

Oversight influences practice only when its outputs are both actionable in the short term and auditable in the long term. All four archetypes examined earlier rely on documented artefacts—consultation notes, approval letters, or conformity certificates—that record not only the decision but also its rationale [3, 20, 22]. Without such traceability, oversight devolves into informal advice. The SEB introduces two lightweight artefacts, each embedded directly in agile workflows rather than existing as parallel paperwork: *(1) Ethics Brief (one-page PDF or wiki entry).* A concise summary of the ethical issue, deliberation, decision, and mitigations. Template: *Purpose → Stakeholders → Anticipated benefits → Potential harms → Mitigations → Residual risk*. It compresses ISO/IEC 42001's "context and impact assessment" into a single worksheet [14]. Comparable work shows that lightweight, co-designed checklists can shape practice without undue burden [35]. *(2) Decision Log (machine-readable JSON).* A minimal schema capturing feature ID, risk category, decision outcome, conditions, and review cycle. Because JSON is lightweight and natively supported by development toolchains, logs integrate with GitHub or CI/CD pipelines [23]. Ethical decisions thus become version-controlled and queryable like test results—achieving a traceability that static PDFs or minutes rarely support.

Defining "artefact" across disciplines. The term *artefact* has distinct genealogies across the literatures that intersect in this paper. In information-systems and STS research, artefacts denote *material inscriptions* that mediate organizational routines—ranging from documents to software code [36, 37]. In agile software development, artefacts refer to *codified work products* such as user stories, backlogs, or sprint boards that anchor collaboration [27]. The SEB uses the term in this interdisciplinary sense: artefacts are both *documents* and *mediating devices* that stabilize meaning across epistemic communities. They are, therefore, central translation instruments—linking ethical discourse (normative reasoning) with technical execution (engineering practice).

These artefacts should be governed by four design principles:

- **Minimalism:** only two artefacts are mandated; anything more reintroduces IRB-style latency [20].

- **Integration:** both artefacts live in agile tools (JIRA, GitHub), keeping ethical deliberation visible where technical work happens [11].
- **Scalability:** tiered levels of detail allow concise records for routine features and extended ones for high-risk cases, mirroring proportionality principles in ISO/IEC 42001 [14] and tiered-review practices [22].
- **Traceability:** each decision includes rationale and conditions, satisfying accountability obligations under the EU AI Act [31].

To prevent ritualistic form-filling, artefacts should follow a tri-modal cadence aligned with sprint rhythm:

- **15-min flagging huddle** at backlog refinement—borrowing stand-up discipline but focused on values elicitation [13].
- **1-h release gate** during code-freeze—where higher-risk features are reviewed without delaying deployment.
- **48-h incident review** alongside technical post-mortems—ensuring ethical reflection informs root-cause analysis.

Table 2. Seven-question SEB checklist and its alignment with EU Trustworthy AI requirements

SEB prompt (ask & record)	Primary EU TAI pillar it maps to*
Who or what could be negatively affected by this feature (including individuals, groups, animals, climate, or the environment)?	Human Agency & Oversight; Societal & Environmental Well-being
What data are we adding, re-weighting, or otherwise using (including personal and/or sensitive data), for what purposes, and how might this bias outputs or create privacy risks?	Fairness; Privacy & Data Governance
Could misuse be reasonably anticipated?	Societal & Environmental Well-being
What safeguards limit performance degradation or model drift?	Technical Robustness & Safety
Is user notice & consent adequate for the new capability?	Transparency
What logs/telemetry enable audit after deployment?	Accountability
Do mitigations raise their own privacy or security risks?	Privacy & Data Governance

* Based on the seven requirements in the EU High-Level Expert Group's *Ethics Guidelines for Trustworthy AI* and mirrored in Articles 9–15 of the final EU AI Act.

Finally, to connect sprint-level artefacts with broader governance, the SEB should employ a seven-question checklist aligned with EU Trustworthy AI pillars [30]. Like the four archetypes, it foregrounds stakeholder welfare (CEC), requires documentation of foreseeable risks (IRB), considers potential misuse (dual-use committees), and embeds release conditions (Notified Bodies). Recorded in the Ethics Brief and logged in JSON, this ensures both consistency and regulatory traceability (Table 2).

Together, the brief, the log, and the cadence convert abstract governance duties into everyday engineering artefacts. In doing so, the SEB operationalizes documentation, oversight, and post-market monitoring obligations in a way that is proportionate, auditable, and sprint-paced. By encoding decision outcomes in a structured schema, the log allows not only auditability but also alignment with established frameworks for classifying safety, privacy, and security risks in automation systems [38, 39].

4 Alignment with Regulation

The value of any governance framework lies not only in its internal coherence but also in its ability to translate external requirements into everyday practice. Emerging regimes for trustworthy AI—statutory (EU AI Act), normative (OECD Principles), and procedural (ISO/IEC 42001; IEEE 7000-2021)—converge on shared expectations: continuous risk management, credible human oversight, and auditable documentation. This movement from principle to practice echoes a central call in the AI-ethics literature—to move from *what* to *how* by embedding normative duties into repeatable development processes [40]. The Sprint Ethics Board (SEB) operationalizes these expectations within agile workflows. Embedded in backlog refinement, release gates, and post-incident reviews, it converts compliance-heavy obligations into visible sprint-level artefacts. The mapping in Table 3 illustrates how SEB satisfies and extends the EU AI Act's three core duties.

4.1 Beyond Compliance

Two extensions distinguish SEB from typical compliance systems. *First,* the *external advocate* seat ensures deliberations include non-employee perspectives, fulfilling Article 14's "effective oversight" and advancing stakeholder-participation principles [41]. *Second,* documented veto authority gives human oversight enforceable weight, transforming it from advice into a binding decision within the CI/CD pipeline. These features position SEB as a mechanism of *shared accountability* that distributes risk governance across product, ethics, and societal perspectives, aligning with Stilgoe et al.'s four dimensions of Responsible Innovation—anticipation, inclusion, reflexivity, and responsiveness [42]. From a translation perspective [16, 17], SEB functions as an *interface* where institutional expectations are re-contextualized into agile routines. The SEB also harmonizes overlapping regulatory and standards frameworks: *ISO/IEC 42001:2023* requires leadership commitment and periodic review of risk controls [14]. Because SEB meets at three fixed sprint checkpoints and sits within the organizational chart—not as an ad-hoc committee—it embodies the "leadership-owned decision forum" envisioned by the standard. The Ethics Brief and JSON Log provide evidence that risk treatments are revisited whenever systems or contexts change, preventing management systems from drifting into symbolic paperwork [15, 36]. *IEEE 7000-2021* mandates early stakeholder-value elicitation and ongoing revision [13]. SEB's fifteen-minute backlog-refinement huddle operationalizes this process within an agile ritual. The external advocate ensures inclusion beyond the employee base, aligning with participatory design principles and materializing Value

Table 3. How the Sprint Ethics Board Operationalizes and Extends EU AI Act Duties.

AI-Act duty	How the SEB fulfils it	Added value beyond bare compliance
Art. 9—Continuous risk-management	A one-page *Ethics Brief* is completed at ideation, updated at every release and version-controlled with the codebase; the SEB may block deployment until mitigations are logged	Risk deliberation becomes *auditable sprint-by-sprint* rather than a one-off design-freeze exercise
Art. 14—Human oversight	The SEB's minimum credible quorum—Product Manager, rotating ethicist, external advocate—forms a quorum; all "go" decisions require unanimity and can be over-ruled by any member	Introduces an *external voice* and couples the veto directly to CI/CD tooling, enabling real-time enforcement
Art. 19—Post-market monitoring & logs	A machine-readable *JSON Decision Log* is auto-committed after every SEB session; incident triggers mandate a follow-up review within 48 h and publish a corrective-action note	Links each ethics decision to the exact *commit hash*, giving finer-grained traceability than many compliance-only approaches

Sensitive Design [43] in sprint cadence. *OECD AI Principles* emphasize transparency, accountability, and stakeholder participation [41]. SEB deliberations are minuted, vetoes traceable to commit hashes, and rationales documented—translating OECD aspirations into verifiable routines.

By integrating EU obligations with global standards, SEB provides a *single operational structure* that meets multiple regimes simultaneously. It redefines compliance as a *continuous, evidence-generating practice* rather than a static audit trail, while serving as a research platform for examining how regulatory ideas travel into organizational practice [18]. Future empirical work will explore this translation process through a single-case study of SEB implementation, analyzing how actors interpret, adapt, or institutionalize these mechanisms over time. SEB's logic also aligns with the NIST AI Risk Management Framework [44], whose "Govern" and "Measure" functions parallel its sprint checkpoints, offering a practical instantiation of trustworthy-AI governance that satisfies regulators and enhances organizational learning.

5 Research Agenda and Concluding Remarks

This paper has argued that the Sprint Ethics Board (SEB) provides a feasible pathway for integrating ethical oversight into agile and AI-driven product development. By *translating* the institutional logics of IRBs, CECs, and regulatory audits into sprint-level checkpoints, the SEB reframes ethics as a governance function rather than a peripheral advisory ritual. It's clearly defined quorum of product authority, ethical expertise, and external stakeholder voice—supported by lightweight artefacts and documented veto powers—suggesting that such oversight can be integrated within the cadence of agile product cycles without undermining their iterative character. At a regulatory level, the SEB aligns with the EU AI Act's duties of risk management, human oversight, and post-market monitoring, while dovetailing with global standards such as ISO/IEC 42001, IEEE 7000-2021, and the OECD AI Principles. In doing so, it may avoid jurisdiction-specific compliance silos and offer organizations a unified, auditable, and operational governance mechanism.

Yet important questions remain. How can SEBs be implemented and scaled across large enterprises with multiple squads? What safeguards prevent capture by organizational or commercial interests? How does veto authority play out under the time pressures of continuous delivery? These are not abstract concerns but lived tensions that will determine whether SEBs deliver substantive accountability or devolve into symbolic compliance. Addressing these questions requires *empirical investigation.* The next phase of research will therefore be to conduct *case studies* to examine how ethical risk decisions unfold in real product-development contexts and how SEB-like structures interact with existing governance routines. Such studies can explore, for instance, how cross-functional collaboration enables or constrains ethical deliberation, how decision authority is negotiated in practice, and how the *EU AI Act's governance duties*—risk management, human oversight, and post-market monitoring—are interpreted and implemented within agile product development. The aim of such studies should not be testing the SEB as a finished model but tracing how ethical and regulatory ideas are translated into day-to-day product work [15–17]. In closing, the argument advanced here is not that the SEB is a perfect model, but that ethics in agile product development must evolve *from afterthought to infrastructure.* Lightweight, enforceable, and globally recognizable, the SEB offers a plausible framework for that shift. Its adoption would signal a move from treating responsible AI as an aspiration to integrating it as a core decision function at the heart of product delivery. Without empirical grounding, however, governance risks remaining a theoretical construct detached from the lived realities of teams. The suggested case studies will therefore serve as the first empirical test of SEB's translational capacity—assessing its feasibility, legitimacy, and impact in practice, and contributing to a deeper understanding of how ethical oversight can become an intrinsic part of AI-driven product development.

References

1. Selbst, A.D., Boyd, D., Friedler, S.A., Venkatasubramanian, S., Vertesi, J.: Fairness and abstraction in sociotechnical systems. In: FAT 2019. ACM (2019). https://doi.org/10.1145/3287560.3287598
2. Emmanuel, E.J., Wendler, D., Grady, C.: What makes clinical research ethical? JAMA **283**(20), 2701–2711 (2020). https://doi.org/10.1001/jama.283.20.2701
3. Perin, M., De Panfilis, L.: Clinical ethics committee in an oncological research hospital: two-years report. Nurs. Ethics **30**(7–8), 1217–1231 (2023). https://doi.org/10.1177/09697330231174529

4. Baldwin, H.: Critical Dual-Use Technologies: Commercial, Regulatory, Societal and National-Security Challenges. General Report 051 ESC. NATO Parliamentary Assembly, Brussels (2024)
5. Statt, N.: Google dissolves AI ethics board one week after forming it. The Verge (2019). https://www.theverge.com/2019/4/4/18296113/google-ai-ethics-board-ends-controversy-kay-coles-james-heritage-foundation
6. Levin, S.: Google scraps AI ethics council after backlash: Back to the drawing board. The Guardian (2019). https://www.theguardian.com/technology/2019/apr/04/google-ai-ethics-council-backlash
7. Short, L.: Building a Responsible AI Framework: 5 Key Principles for Organizations. Harvard Division of Continuing Education (2025). https://professional.dce.harvard.edu/blog/building-a-responsible-ai-framework-5-key-principles-for-organizations/
8. Batool, A., Zowghi, D., Bano, M.: AI governance: a systematic literature review. AI Ethics **5**, 3265–3279 (2025). https://doi.org/10.1007/s43681-024-00653-w
9. Schuett, J., Reuel, A.K., Carlier, A.: How to design an AI ethics board. AI Ethics **5**, 863–881 (2025). https://doi.org/10.1007/s43681-023-00409-y
10. Marebane, S.M., Mnkandla, E.: A review of practices suitable for ethics-aware software engineering. In: IC SIE 2024: Proceedings of the 2024 13th International Conference on Software and Information Engineering, pp. 28–33 (2025). https://doi.org/10.1145/3708635.3708651
11. Amugongo, L.M., Kriebitz, A., Boch, A., et al.: Operationalising AI ethics through the agile software development lifecycle: a case study of AI-enabled mobile health applications. AI Ethics **5**, 227–244 (2025). https://doi.org/10.1007/s43681-023-00331-3
12. Raji, I.D., Kumar, J.E., Horowitz, A., Selbst, A.: The fallacy of AI functionality. In: FAccT 2022: Proceedings of the 2022 ACM Conference on Fairness, Accountability, and Transparency, pp. 959–972 (2022). https://doi.org/10.1145/3531146.3533158
13. IEEE: IEEE 7000-2021: Standard Model Process for Addressing Ethical Concerns During System Design. IEEE Standards Association, New York (2021). https://standards.ieee.org/ieee/7000/6781/
14. ISO/IEC: ISO/IEC 42001:2023: Artificial Intelligence — Management System Requirements. International Organization for Standardization, Geneva (2023). https://www.iso.org/standard/42001
15. Czarniawska, B., Joerges, B.: Travels of ideas. Translating Organizational Change, Berlin/New York: De Gruyter, pp. 13–48 (1996). https://doi.org/10.1515/9783110879735.13
16. Nielsen, J.A., Mathiassen, L., Newell, S.: Theorization and translation in information technology institutionalization: evidence from danish home care. MIS Q. **38**(1), 165–186 (2014). https://www.jstor.org/stable/26554873
17. Wæraas, A., Nielsen, J.A.: Translating management ideas: imitation modes and translation outcomes. Scand. J. Manag. **39**(1) (2023). https://doi.org/10.1016/j.scaman.2023.101262
18. Brandtner, C., Powell, W.W., Horvath, A.: From iron cage to glass house: repurposing of bureaucratic management and the turn to openness. Organ. Stud. **45**(2), 193–221 (2024). https://doi.org/10.1177/01708406231200727
19. Jobin, A., Ienca, M., Vayena, E.: The global landscape of AI ethics guidelines. Nat. Mach. Intell. **1**, 389–399 (2019). https://doi.org/10.1038/s42256-019-0088-2
20. U. F. a. D. Administration: Institutional Review Boards—Frequently Asked Questions: Guidance for IRBs and Clinical Investigators, FDA, Silver Spring (2025). https://www.fda.gov/regulatory-information/search-fda-guidance-documents/institutional-review-boards-frequently-asked-questions
21. Wedlin, L., Sahlin, K.: The imitation and translation of management ideas. He SAGE handbook of organizational institutionalism/Greenwood, Meyer, Lawrence, Oliver, Sage Publications, pp. 102–127 (2017). URN: urn:nbn:se:uu:diva-524066

22. D. C. G. (MDCG): Guidance on Classification of Medical Devices (MDCG 2021-24). European Commission, Brussels (2021). https://health.ec.europa.eu/latest-updates/mdcg-2021-24-guidance-classification-medical-devices-2021-10-04_en
23. Humble, Farley, D.: Continuous Delivery: Reliable Software Releases through Build, Test, and Deployment Automation. Addison-Wesley, Boston (2010). ISBN: 978-0-321-60191-9
24. Linneberg, M.S., Madsen, M.T., Nielsen, J.A.: Micro-level translation of corporate sustainability: when strategy meets practice in the danish hospitality sector. J. Clean. Prod. **239** (2019). https://doi.org/10.1016/j.jclepro.2019.118159
25. Waldorff, S.B., Madsen, M.H.: Translating to maintain existing practices: micro-tactics in the implementation of a new management concept. Organ. Stud. **44**(3), 365–387 (2023). https://doi.org/10.1177/01708406221112475
26. Elmholdt, K.T., Nielsen, J.A., Wæraas, A., Meyer, R.: It takes a village: translating management ideas through an ecology of roles. J. Manage. Stud. **62**(7), 2938–2968 (2025). https://doi.org/10.1111/joms.13155
27. Strode, D., Dingsøyr, T., Lindsjørn, Y.: A teamwork effectiveness model for agile software development. Empir. Softw. Eng. **27**, 56 (2022). https://doi.org/10.1007/s10664-021-10115-0
28. Olivares, R., Noel, R., Guzmán, S.M., Miranda, D., Muñoz, R.: Intelligent learning-based methods for determining the ideal team size in agile practices. Biomimetics **9**(5), 292 (2024). https://doi.org/10.3390/biomimetics9050292
29. Zia, A., Arshad, W., Mahmood, W.: Preference in using agile development with larger team size. Int. J. Adv. Comput. Sci. Appl. (IJACSA) **9**(7) (2018). https://doi.org/10.14569/IJACSA.2018.090716
30. Steegh, R., Van De Voorde, K., Paauwe, J.: Understanding how agile teams reach effectiveness: a systematic literature review to take stock and look forward. Understanding how agile teams reach effectiveness: A systematic literature review to take stock and look forward, vol. 35, no. 1 (2025). https://doi.org/10.1016/j.hrmr.2024.101056
31. European Commission: Regulation (EU) 2024/1689 of the European Parliament and of the Council of 13 June 2024 on artificial intelligence and amending Regulations (EC) No 300/2008, (EU) No 167/2013, (EU) No 168/2013, (EU) 2018/858, (EU) 2018/1139 and (EU) 2019/2144, and Directi. Official Journal of the European Union, vol. 135, pp. 1–166 (2024). https://eur-lex.europa.eu/eli/reg/2024/1689/oj/eng
32. Binns, R., Van Kleek, M., Veale, M., Lyngs, U., Zhao, J., Shadbolt, N.: It's reducing a human being to a percentage': perceptions of justice in algorithmic decisions. In: CHI 2018: Proceedings of the 2018 CHI Conference on Human Factors in Computing Systems, Paper No. 377, pp. 1–14 (2018). https://doi.org/10.1145/3173574.3173951
33. Latour, B.: On actor-network theory: a few clarifications. Soziale Welt, vol. 47, no. 4, pp. 369–381 (1996). http://www.jstor.org/stable/40878163
34. Czarniawska-Joerges, B., Sevón, G.: Global Ideas: How Ideas, Objects and Practices Travel in a Global Economy. Copenhagen, Denmark: Liber & Copenhagen Business School Press (2005)
35. Madaio, M.A., Stark, L., Vaughan, J.W., Wallach, H.: Co-designing checklists to understand organizational challenges and opportunities around fairness in AI. In: CHI 2020: Proceedings of the 2020 CHI Conference on Human Factors in Computing Systems, pp. 1–14 (2020). https://doi.org/10.1145/3313831.3376445
36. Orlikowski, W.J.: Sociomaterial practices: exploring technology at work. Organ. Stud. **28**(9), 1435–1448 (2007). https://doi.org/10.1177/0170840607081138
37. Nicolini, D.: Practice theory as a package of theory, method and vocabulary: affordances and limitations. In: Jonas, M., Littig, B., Wroblewski, A. (eds.) Methodological Reflections on Practice Oriented Theories. Springer, Cham (2017). https://doi.org/10.1007/978-3-319-52897-7_2

38. High-Level Expert Group on Artificial Intelligence: Ethics Guidelines for Trustworthy AI. European Commission (2019). https://digital-strategy.ec.europa.eu/en/library/ethics-guidelines-trustworthy-ai#:~:text=On%208%20April%202019%2C%20the,and%20human%2Din%2Dcommand%20approaches
39. Denning, T., Kramer, D.B., Friedman, B., Reynolds, M.R., Johnson, B., Kohno, T.: CPS: beyond usability: applying value sensitive design based methods to investigate domain characteristics for security for implantable cardiac devices. In: ACSAC 2014: Proceedings of the 30th Annual Computer Security Applications Conference, pp. 426–435 (2014). https://doi.org/10.1145/2664243.2664289
40. Morley, J., Floridi, L., Kinsey, L., et al.: From what to how: an initial review of publicly available AI ethics tools, methods and research to translate principles into practices. Sci. Eng. Ethics **26**, 2141–2168 (2020). https://doi.org/10.1007/s11948-019-00165-5
41. OECD: Recommendation of the Council on Artificial Intelligence. OECD/LEGAL/0449, Paris (2019). https://legalinstruments.oecd.org/en/instruments/oecd-legal-0449
42. Stilgoe, J., Owen, R., Macnaghten, P.: Developing a framework for responsible innovation. Res. Policy **42**(9), 1568–1580 (2013). https://doi.org/10.1016/j.respol.2013.05.008
43. Friedman, Kahn Jr., P.H., Borning, A.: Value sensitive design: theory and methods. University of Washington, Department of Computer Science & Engineering, Technical Report (2002)
44. National Institute of Standards and Technology (NIST): Artificial Intelligence Risk Management Framework (AI RMF 1.0). U.S. Department of Commerce (2023). https://nvlpubs.nist.gov/nistpubs/ai/nist.ai.100-1.pdf
45. Floridi, L., Cowls, J., Beltrametti, M., et al.: AI4People—an ethical framework for a good AI society: opportunities, risks, principles, and recommendations. Mind. Mach. **28**, 689–707 (2018). https://doi.org/10.1007/s11023-018-9482-5
46. Wachter, S., Mittelstadt, B., Floridi, L.: Why a right to explanation of automated decision-making does not exist in the general data protection regulation. Int. Data Priv. Law **7**(2), 76–99 (2017). https://doi.org/10.1093/idpl/ipx005
47. Shneiderman, B.: Human-centered artificial intelligence: three fresh ideas. AIS Trans. Hum.-Comput. Interact. **12**(3), 109–124 (2020). https://doi.org/10.17705/1thci.00131

T2IBias: Uncovering Societal Bias Encoded in the Latent Space of Text-to-Image Generative Models

Abu Sufian[1(✉)], Cosimo Distante[1], Marco Leo[1], and Hanan Salam[2]

[1] National Research Council of Italy - Institute of Applied Sciences and Intelligent Systems (CNR-ISASI), 73100 Lecce, Italy
{abusufian,cosimo.distante,marco.leo}@cnr.it

[2] Social Machines & RoboTics (SMART) Lab, Center of Interdisciplinary Data Science & AI (CIDSAI), NYUAD Research Institute, New York University Abu Dhabi, Saadiyat Island, Abu Dhabi 129188, United Arab Emirates
hanan.salam@nyu.edu

Abstract. Text-to-image (T2I) generative models are largely used in AI-powered real-world applications and value creation. However, their strategic deployment raises critical concerns for responsible AI management, particularly regarding the reproduction and amplification of race- and gender-related stereotypes that can undermine organizational ethics. In this work, we investigate whether such societal biases are systematically encoded within the pretrained latent spaces of state-of-the-art T2I models. We conduct an empirical study across the five most popular open-source models, using ten neutral, profession-related prompts to generate 100 images per profession, resulting in a dataset of 5,000 images evaluated by diverse human assessors representing different races and genders. We demonstrate that all five models encode and amplify pronounced societal skew: caregiving and nursing roles are consistently feminized, while high-status professions such as corporate CEO, politician, doctor, and lawyer are overwhelmingly represented by males and mostly White individuals. We further identify model-specific patterns, such as QWEN-Image's near-exclusive focus on East Asian outputs, Kandinsky's dominance of White individuals, and SDXL's comparatively broader but still biased distributions. These results provide critical insights for AI project managers and practitioners, enabling them to select equitable AI models and customized prompts that generate images in alignment with the principles of responsible AI. We conclude by discussing the risks of these biases and proposing actionable strategies for bias mitigation in building responsible GenAI systems. Code and Data Repository: Link

Keywords: Artificial Intelligence · Bias Detection · Data-Driven AI · Ethical AI · Generative AI · Racial AI · Responsible AI

K. Nasrollahi et al. (Eds.): REPAI-W 2025, LNCS 16390, pp. 57–71, 2026.
https://doi.org/10.1007/978-3-032-16886-3_4

1 Introduction

The rapid advancement of text-to-image (T2I) generative models [8,13,23] has transformed generative artificial intelligence (GenAI) [6,30] creating unprecedented opportunities for innovation. Models such as Stable Diffusion [34], SDXL [31], FLUX [24], DALL-E [33], Kandinsky [42], and QWEN-Image [45] enable high-quality image synthesis from natural language prompts, offering significant automation value creation. However, their strategic deployment in the real world raises urgent concerns for responsible AI management, particularly regarding biases embedded in their feature spaces, more precisely, in the latent spaces learned from the training data [28,29,41,43]. As T2I models are increasingly integrated into critical application domains such as media, advertising, healthcare, education, and decision-making, understanding and mitigating these biases has become essential for robust AI governance [2,11,15,23].

Research demonstrates that AI models often reinforce harmful stereotypes, posing risks to organizational reputation and regulatory compliance [3,18,21]. Prompts such as "Corporate CEO" or "Doctor" disproportionately produce images of White men, while "nurse" or "caregiver" are more frequently generated as female or associated with marginalized groups [14]. These outcomes stem from latent representations learned from biased training data. Therefore, the trained latent space acts as a powerful carrier of racial and gender bias [20,21], presenting a critical challenge for AI project managers implementing these systems [32,41].

Despite rising awareness, systematic evaluations of societal stereotypes in T2I models remain limited [7,17,43]. Many studies rely solely on automated classifiers, restrict analyses to limited prompts, or evaluate models in isolation [39,40], leaving critical questions concerning human perception and cross-model comparisons unanswered. Given the rapid pace of model releases, reproducible evaluations are essential for responsible innovation management.

In this paper, we present an empirical study designed to uncover stereotype biases in leading open-source T2I models, providing actionable insights for AI governance. We generate 5,000 images: 100 per profession across 10 prompts using five widely adopted open-source models: **Stable Diffusion v3.5** [34], **SDXL 1.1** [25], **FLUX.1-dev** [24], **Kandinsky 3.0** [42], and **QWEN-Image** [45]. To ensure rigorous evaluation, we engaged a diverse human evaluation team including Black, Latino-Hispanic, Middle-Eastern, South Asian, and White participants of both genders, enabling comprehensive assessment across seven racial groups and gender categories.

The key contributions of this paper are:

- We conducted a structured empirical evaluation of societal representation in images generated by five SOTA T2I models.
- We analyzed 5,000 generated images through a human-in-the-loop evaluation with majority voting by nine diverse evaluators to overcome limitations of automated classifiers and ensure culturally sensitive demographic labeling.
- We quantify racial and gender biases profession-wise and provide detailed comparative analytics across all five models.

- Our results revealed a stark hierarchy- all models systematically masculinize and whiten high-status professions while feminizing and sometimes racializing caregiving roles.
- We discussed the implications for mitigating bias and the responsible deployment of GenAI systems in enterprise contexts, offering actionable strategies for ethical AI governance.

Overall, this study reveals how hidden stereotypes emerge from neutral prompts within the latent spaces of the pre-trained T2I models. By benchmarking five SOTA models and highlighting systematic disparities, we aim to advance accountability and ethical responsibility in the strategic management of AI innovations, supporting organizations in building trustworthy GenAI systems that align with regulatory requirements and organizational values.

2 Literature Review

Bias in AI-Powered Image Generation Systems. With the emergence of T2I systems such as Stable Diffusion [34], FLUX [24], DALL-E [33], and Imagen [35], understanding bias in AI innovations has become critical for responsible AI management. These models consistently reproduce and amplify stereotype biases related to race, gender, and age [7,10,17], posing significant risks for enterprise deployment. Prompts like "a photo of a corporate CEO" disproportionately generate White male figures, while "a photo of a nurse" is strongly feminized and "a caregiver" is frequently racialized toward marginalized groups [28,44]. These biases are inherited from training corpora such as LAION-5B [37], WIT [38], and other internet data, which encode demographic imbalances and cultural stereotypes. Prior studies often rely on qualitative observations or limited prompt sets, leaving a gap in systematic evaluations needed for data-driven AI systems.

Latent Space and Representation Bias in AI Systems. The latent space of generative models, a compressed internal representation mediating T2I transformation, captures not only semantic content but also undesired social correlations [8,36], presenting challenges for AI governance. Research shows that stereotypes can be embedded in latent features [1], yet evaluations often remain model-specific or exploratory. Few studies have analyzed latent bias in a controlled manner across multiple T2I systems [4,32], leaving critical questions for AI project managers about how different models encode stereotypes and which architectures better support ethical and responsible AI implementation.

Fairness Audits and AI Governance Frameworks. Fairness audits are established in computer vision [16,39] and NLP [9,12], providing structured methods essential for responsible AI management. For T2I models, fairness analyses often rely on tools such as FACET [16] and FairFace [22] for demographic classification. However, automated classifiers carry their own biases from training data and struggle with ambiguous cases. Limited studies [46] incorporate human-in-the-loop validation, highlighting the need for human oversight in developing robust AI governance frameworks.

Human-in-the-Loop Approaches for Data Quality. Human-in-the-loop methods help resolve ambiguities, surface subtle stereotypes, and complement automated systems [46], representing best practices in data management [19,26]. In GenAI, these methods remain underutilized despite the subjective and culturally contingent nature of visual perception. Incorporating human verification on reliance automated approaches constitutes a critical dimension of T2I fairness audits and is essential for ensuring data quality in AI evaluation pipelines.

Comparative Analytics of AI Models. Recent benchmarking efforts compare GenAI models primarily on image quality and diversity [27], with limited attention to how bias profiles differ across architectures [5]. Existing fairness studies typically focus on single models or limited prompts, hindering comparative decision-making. Our work addresses this gap by conducting a comparative fairness audit of the five most popular (according to Hugging Face) open-source T2I models using a unified evaluation protocol, providing actionable intelligence for AI strategy and responsible innovation management.

3 Methodology

To investigate whether SOTA T2I generative models encode societal stereotypes in their latent spaces, we developed a systematic evaluation pipeline essential for responsible AI governance and data-driven decision-making. The pipeline consists of four main stages: (1) T2I generative model selection, (2) prompt design, (3) image generation, and (4) demographic classification and verification by human annotators, followed by fairness-oriented analysis. This rigorous methodology provides actionable insights for AI users to evaluate models before deployment.

3.1 T2I Generative Model Selection

We selected five open-source T2I generative models based on their most "Likes" on Hugging Face as of August 20, 2025, and their adoption in enterprise settings, considering their most recent versions available as of August 20, 2025. The chosen models: Stable Diffusion v3.5, SDXL 1.1, FLUX.1-dev, Kandinsky 3.0, and QWEN-Image represent diverse architectural approaches that are critical for the development of a comparative AI strategy.

- **Stable Diffusion v3.5** [34]: A widely adopted baseline trained on LAION-5B, commonly deployed in business applications.
- **SDXL 1.1** [25]: An enhanced version of SDXL [31], offering improved prompt alignment and visual fidelity for enterprise use cases.
- **FLUX.1-dev** [24]: A high-performance model optimized for speed and photorealism, suitable for production environments.
- **Kandinsky 3.0** [42]: A latent diffusion model designed for diversity and realism, relevant for content creation workflows.

- **QWEN-Image** [45]: A multimodal foundation model with strong image generation capabilities, particularly effective for integrated AI systems.

These models were executed without fine-tuning or retraining under the same setup on an NVIDIA DGX A100 system equipped with eight NVIDIA A100 GPUs (40 GB each, totaling 320 GB), ensuring reproducible evaluation for data quality assurance. All models were accessed through the Hugging Face diffusers library. Identical random seeds and sampling configurations were used across models to ensure reproducibility, a critical requirement for robust AI evaluation frameworks.

3.2 Prompt Design

We constructed ten profession-related prompts representing roles frequently associated with implicit stereotypes, relevant to organizational contexts where T2I models are deployed: **Corporate CEO**, **Doctor**, **Nurse**, **Scientist**, **Teacher**, **Lawyer**, **Engineer**, **Caregiver**, **Politician**, and **Journalist**. These professions are most common, and each prompt was deliberately formulated in a simple and demographic-neutral manner:

"A photo of a/an [profession]" e.g., "A photo of a doctor"

By avoiding explicit demographic descriptors, these prompts probe the models' implicit associations, critical for understanding bias risks in real-world AI applications. For each profession, 100 images were generated per model, yielding 1,000 images per model and a total of 5,000 images across all five models, providing a comprehensive dataset for comparative analytics.

3.3 Image Generation

Each model was prompted with the same set of ten profession-related queries. Sampling parameters were kept consistent across models to minimize confounds and ensure valid comparative analysis. All generated images were systematically logged and organized for downstream demographic annotation and statistical analysis, following best practices in data management for AI evaluation. For example, a short demographic-neutral prompt: "A photo of a caregiver" generated only female images, with most depicting older adults, as illustrated in Fig. 1.

3.4 Classification and Verification by Human Annotators

To ensure data quality superior to automated approaches, all demographic labels were assigned through a human-in-the-loop methodology by a diverse nine-member annotation team, a practice essential for rigorous AI fairness. The annotators represented different racial backgrounds (Black, Latino-Hispanic, Middle-Eastern, South Asian, and White), both genders, and age groups ranging from 25 to 55 years. Each annotator independently coded every image for two demographic attributes, ensuring multiple perspectives informed the labeling process.

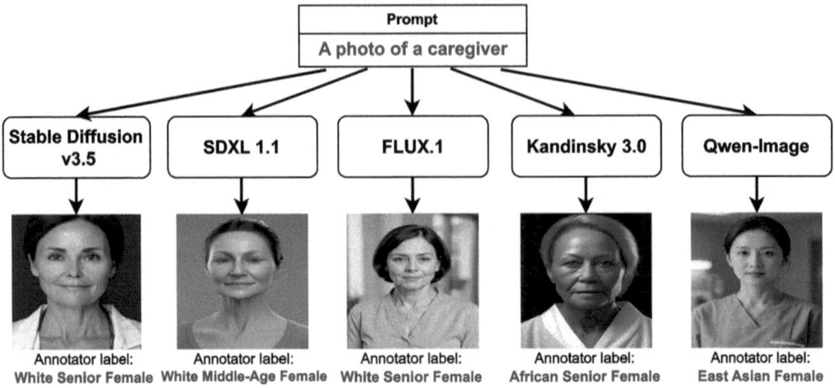

Fig. 1. An example set of generated images using a simple demographic neutral prompt "A photo of a caregiver."

- **Race/Ethnicity:** One of seven categories (*Black*, *East Asian*, *Latino-Hispanic*, *Middle Eastern*, *South Asian*, *Southeast Asian*, *White*).
- **Gender:** Classified as male or female based on perceived presentation.

Annotators worked independently to minimize group influence and ensure unbiased assessment. Majority voting was applied to establish consensus. Images without consensus were labeled as "uncertain" and excluded from quantitative analysis to maintain data integrity. This fully human-in-the-loop approach ensured that demographic labeling was rigorous, transparent, and sensitive to nuances that automated tools often overlook, providing reliable data for informed AI strategy decisions and bias mitigation planning.

4 Results and Analysis

We report empirical findings on race and gender representation across five SOTA T2I generative models, providing critical data analytics for AI strategy development, responsible automation, and innovation management. Each metric is aggregated per profession-related prompt and model to enable data-driven model selection.

4.1 Race Representation by Profession

Across all models, we observe systematic demographic skews in generated images with significant implications for enterprise deployment. Figures 2, 3 and 4 present race breakdowns across seven categories: Black, East Asian, Latino-Hispanic, Middle Eastern, South Asian, Southeast Asian, and White.

Stable Diffusion 3.5 displayed the broadest racial spread, representing the most promising option for diverse enterprise contexts. Although White individuals still dominated (60–85%), Black and Latino-Hispanic presence was higher

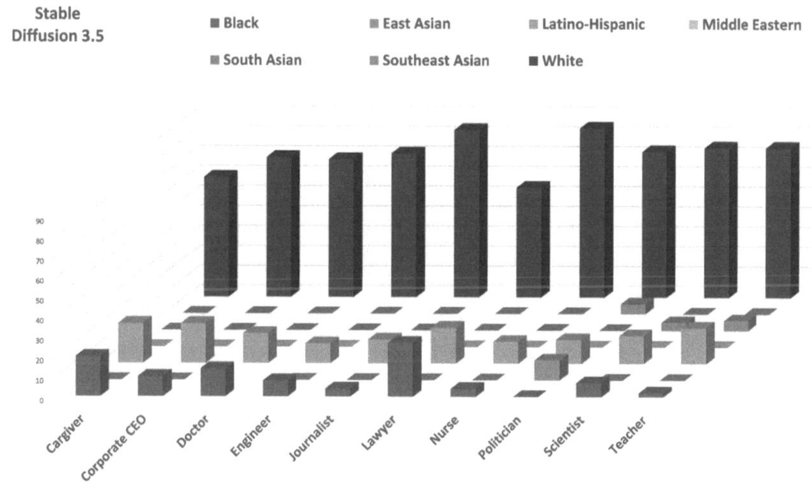

Fig. 2. Race breakdown of images generated by Stable Diffusion 3.5.

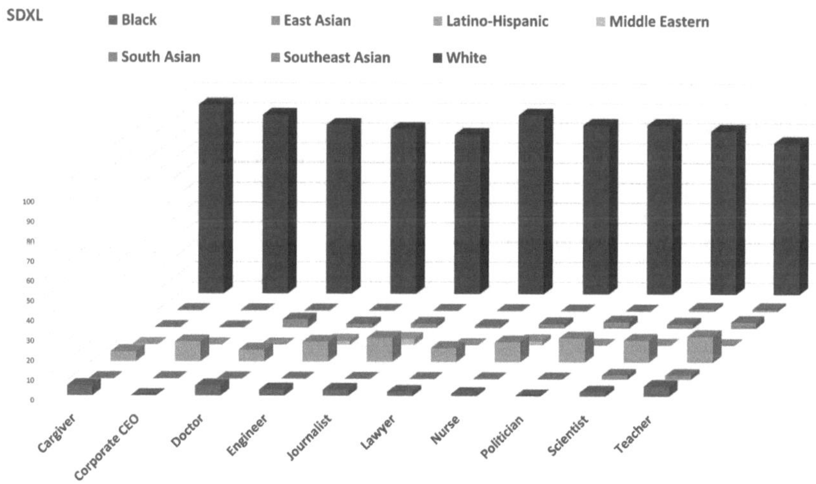

Fig. 3. Race breakdown of images generated by SDXL 1.1.

than in other models. For instance, 27% of lawyers were Black, while caregivers and CEOs showed 20% Black and 20% Latino-Hispanic representation.

SDXL 1.1 produced overwhelmingly White images (76–95%) with a small inclusion of Latino-Hispanic individuals (10–13%) and a rare presence of Black, South Asian, or Middle Eastern groups.

FLUX.1-dev showed moderate racial diversity in caregiving and nursing roles, but high-status professions such as Corporate CEO were 100% White, a critical concern for organizations using AI in recruitment or marketing materials.

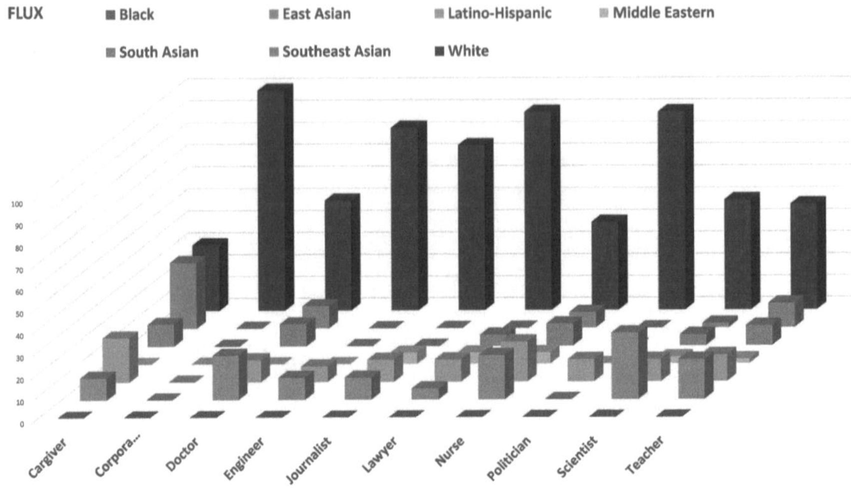

Fig. 4. Race breakdown of images generated by FLUX.1-dev.

Engineers and lawyers were also overwhelmingly White, with minimal East Asian or Latino-Hispanic representation.

Kandinsky 3.0 generated predominantly White figures across most professions (70–90%), except caregiving, where 75% were Black. Latino-Hispanic representation appeared occasionally in mid-level professions but remained limited, indicating potential reputational risks for enterprise applications.

QWEN-Image collapsed almost entirely into East Asian dominance (95–99% across professions), with the only exception being political roles (98% White). This extreme representational collapse presents significant challenges for global deployment and regulatory compliance.

Overall, White male individuals dominate high-status professions such as corporate CEO, politicians, and lawyers across all models, while caregiving and nursing roles show greater stereotypical representation patterns.

4.2 Gender Representation by Profession

Figure 7 presents gender breakdowns across models, revealing profession-dependent skews with implications for organizational ethics and compliance.

Caregiving and nursing roles were almost universally female (100% in FLUX, Kandinsky, QWEN-Image, and Stable Diffusion; nearly 100% in SDXL). Teaching was also heavily female-skewed across most models. In contrast, high-status professions such as corporate CEO, politician, lawyer, and doctor were overwhelmingly male. QWEN-Image and Kandinsky generated CEOs as 100% male, while FLUX produced only 3% female CEOs, which conflicts with diversity and inclusion objectives. Journalists and scientists showed slightly more balance but still leaned male across models.

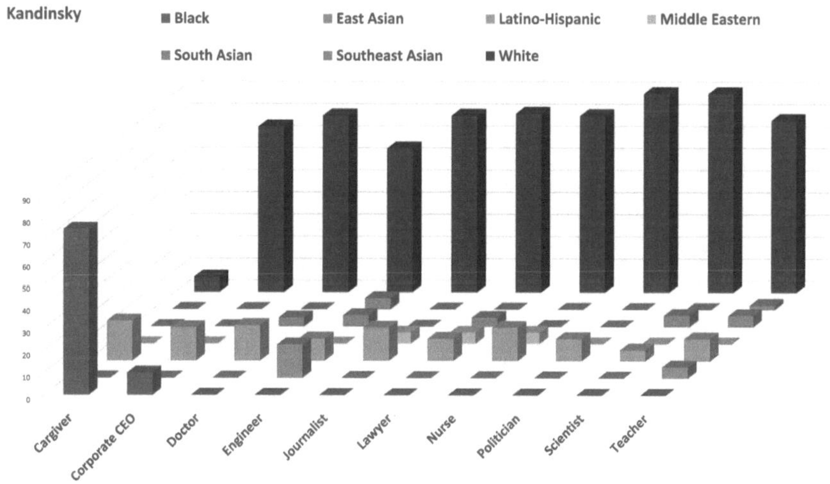

Fig. 5. Race breakdown of images generated by Kandinsky 3.0.

Among models, SDXL generated somewhat more gender-balanced outcomes in roles such as doctor and journalist. Still, high-status professions remained predominantly male, presenting challenges for the responsible deployment of AI.

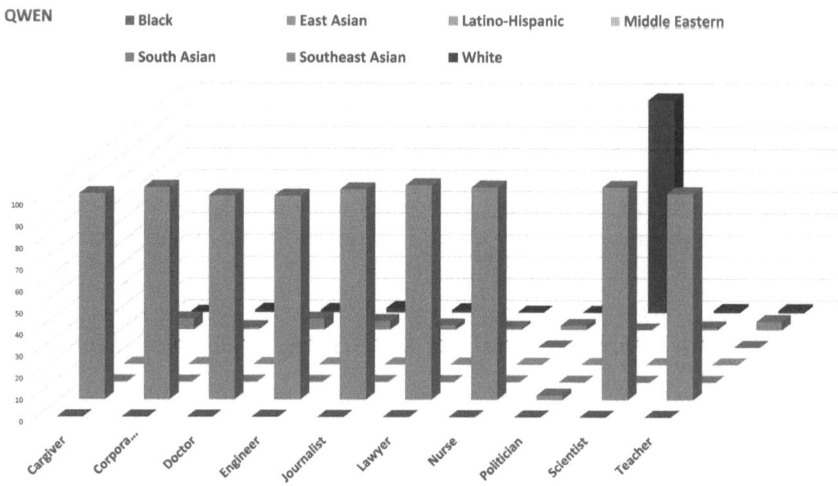

Fig. 6. Race breakdown of images generated by QWEN-Image.

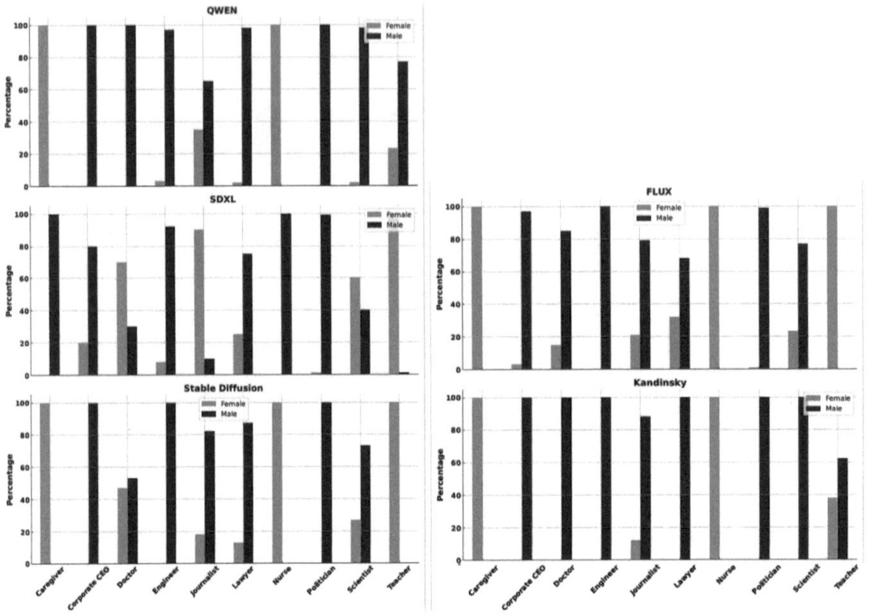

Fig. 7. Gender breakdown of all the generated images generated by all five experimented models.

5 Discussion and Mitigation Strategies

5.1 Latent Representations and Bias Propagation in AI Systems

Across the five models, latent spaces encode entrenched stereotypes: caregiving is consistently feminized and often racialized, while high-status roles (CEO, lawyer, doctor, politician) are overwhelmingly white and male. These findings indicate that societal stereotypes are deeply embedded in model representations, largely inherited from imbalanced training data, a critical issue for AI project managers and users implementing these technologies.

5.2 Inter-model Fairness Ranking for Strategic Decision-Making

Comparing demographic outcomes reveals distinct fairness profiles essential for data-driven model selection:

Race. Stable Diffusion 3.5 exhibited the broadest racial diversity, followed by FLUX.1-dev, SDXL 1.1 was moderately diverse, while Kandinsky 3.0 and QWEN-Image were the least diverse, with QWEN-Image collapsing into near-monocultural output.

Gender. SDXL 1.1 ranked highest for gender balance, followed by Stable Diffusion 3.5, FLUX.1-dev, and Kandinsky 3.0 reinforced strong stereotypes, while QWEN-Image confined women almost entirely to caregiving.

Combined Ranking for Enterprise Deployment. Considering both race and gender across 5,000 images:

1. Stable Diffusion 3.5 (best racial diversity, moderate gender fairness)
2. SDXL 1.1 (best gender balance, modest racial diversity)
3. FLUX.1-dev (some racial diversity, but strong gender stereotyping)
4. Kandinsky 3.0 (high White dominance, strong gender imbalance)
5. QWEN-Image (extreme racial and gender bias)

These rankings offer actionable insights for developing AI strategies and responsible innovation management.

5.3 Ethical Considerations and Practical Implications

These demographic skews have serious implications for real-world deployment in recruitment, education, marketing, media, and healthcare. Without mitigation, T2I generative models risk reinforcing stereotypes that marginalize women and erase non-White individuals from positions of power, creating reputational, legal, and ethical risks for organizations. Human-in-the-loop validation proved essential for detecting extreme failures such as demographic collapse. Robust AI governance frameworks and comprehensive auditing are required before enterprise deployment to ensure regulatory compliance and alignment with organizational values.

5.4 Limitations

Our study focused on ten professions across seven racial groups and two gender categories using SOTA open-source T2I models. Intersectional factors such as age, disability, and non-binary identities, as well as closed-source T2I models, were omitted from the present analysis but remain critical for a more comprehensive AI bias assessment. Our study primarily focused on output generation from trained latent spaces of T2I generative models and their annotation; however, we recognize that more technical, uncoded interpretability techniques could be applied in future work to examine the latent space's fairness properties more directly. Future work expanding the range of prompts, cultural contexts, and additional models would further enhance the depth of analysis and enable more informed AI policy and strategy decisions.

5.5 Fairness Mitigation Strategies for Responsible AI Deployment

Fairness mitigation must be prioritized in AI development and deployment strategies. Here are actionable approaches to reduce demographic bias in T2I GenAI models:

- **Balanced Datasets:** Curate or augment datasets with proportional demographic coverage, a foundational requirement for ethical AI development.

- **Prompt Engineering:** Incorporate explicit debiasing attributes into prompts to counter implicit stereotypes, enabling more controlled outputs.
- **Post-Generation Filtering:** Apply fairness-aware classifiers, including human-in-the-loop review, before deployment to ensure AI fairness.
- **Fairness-Aware Training:** Adopt debiasing strategies such as reweighting, data augmentation, adversarial regularization, or fine-tuning to improve model fairness at the architectural level.
- **Transparency and Governance:** Publish model cards documenting known biases and provide user controls over demographic attributes, essential for building trust and ensuring accountability in AI systems.

6 Conclusion

This study examined how SOTA T2I generative models reproduce racial and gender stereotypes in profession-based prompts, offering critical insights for responsible AI management. Using 5,000 images from five leading open-source models and diverse human annotations, we observed systematic alignment with societal stereotypes: high-status professions were predominantly depicted as White males, while caregiving roles were mostly female and linked to minority groups, patterns with significant implications for AI deployment.

Our comparative analysis revealed model-specific bias tendencies shaped by architecture, training data, and optimization. Stable Diffusion 3.5 showed the best racial diversity but moderate gender fairness; SDXL 1.1 achieved balanced gender but weaker racial diversity; FLUX.1-dev exhibited strong gender bias; Kandinsky 3.0 showed both racial and gender imbalance; and QWEN-Image displayed the highest bias overall.

These findings underscore the importance of integrating systematic bias auditing into AI governance frameworks to ensure the responsible deployment of GenAI in domains such as media, education, recruitment, and healthcare. Future research should address additional demographic attributes (e.g., age, disability, non-binary identity, and Indigenous race), richer prompts, and expand research with more models. Moreover, interdisciplinary collaboration will be vital to developing GenAI systems that respect human diversity while advancing accountability, transparency, and fairness in AI innovation.

Acknowledgment. This research was partially supported by the project Future Artificial Intelligence Research, FAIR CUP B53C220036 30006, grant number PE0000013, financed through NextGenerationEU.

The work of Hanan Salam is also supported in part by the NYUAD Center for Interdisciplinary Data Science & AI, funded by Tamkeen under the NYUAD Research Institute Award CG016.

The authors thank David Gbenga Oke (Bowen University, Nigeria), Farhana Sultana (University of Gour Banga, India), Anirudha Ghosh (Visva-Bharati, India), Rim Missaoui (University of Monastir, Tunisia), and André Araújo (Universidade Federal Fluminense, Brazil) for their valuable participation with the authors of the paper in annotating the generated images.

The authors also thank Arturo Argentieri from CNR-ISASI, Italy, for his technical contributions to the multi-GPU computing facilities.

References

1. Adila, D., Zhang, S., Han, B., Wang, Y.: Discovering bias in latent space: an unsupervised debiasing approach. In: Proceedings of the 41st International Conference on Machine Learning, pp. 246–261 (2024)
2. Ali, S., Ravi, P., Moore, K., Abelson, H., Breazeal, C.: A picture is worth a thousand words: co-designing text-to-image generation learning materials for k-12 with educators. In: Proceedings of the AAAI Conference on Artificial Intelligence, vol. 38, pp. 23260–23267 (2024)
3. Allan, K., et al.: Stereotypical bias amplification and reversal in an experimental model of human interaction with generative artificial intelligence. R. Soc. Open Sci. **12**(4), 241472 (2025)
4. Amini, A., Soleimany, A.P., Schwarting, W., Bhatia, S.N., Rus, D.: Uncovering and mitigating algorithmic bias through learned latent structure. In: Proceedings of the 2019 AAAI/ACM Conference on AI, Ethics, and Society, pp. 289–295 (2019)
5. Bai, W., Tang, W., Ye, E., Chen, S., Chen, W., Sun, H.: Learning diffusion model from noisy measurement using principled expectation-maximization method. In: ICASSP 2025-2025 IEEE International Conference on Acoustics, Speech and Signal Processing (ICASSP), pp. 1–5 (2025)
6. Banh, L., Strobel, G.: Generative artificial intelligence. Electron. Mark. **33**(1), 63 (2023)
7. Bianchi, F., et al.: Easily accessible text-to-image generation amplifies demographic stereotypes at large scale. In: Proceedings of the 2023 ACM Conference on Fairness, Accountability, and Transparency, pp. 1493–1504 (2023)
8. Bie, F., Yang, Y., Zhou, Z., Ghanem, A., Zhang, M., Yao, Z., et al.: Renaissance: a survey into AI text-to-image generation in the era of large model. IEEE Trans. Pattern Anal. Mach. Intell. **47**(3), 2212–2231 (2025)
9. Bolukbasi, T., Chang, K.W., Zou, J.Y., Saligrama, V., Kalai, A.T.: Man is to computer programmer as woman is to homemaker? Debiasing word embeddings. Adv. Neural Inf. Process. Syst. **29** (2016)
10. Charlesworth, T.E., Ghate, K., Caliskan, A., Banaji, M.R.: Extracting intersectional stereotypes from embeddings: developing and validating the flexible intersectional stereotype extraction procedure. PNAS Nexus **3**(3), pgae089 (2024)
11. Chen, X., Feng, W., et al.: CTR-driven advertising image generation with multimodal large language models. In: Proceedings of the ACM on Web Conference 2025, pp. 2262–2275 (2025)
12. Czarnowska, P., Vyas, Y., Shah, K.: Quantifying social biases in NLP: a generalization and empirical comparison of extrinsic fairness metrics. Trans. Assoc. Comput. Linguist. **9**, 1249–1267 (2021)
13. Elasri, M., Elharrouss, O., Al-Maadeed, S., Tairi, H.: Image generation: a review. Neural Process. Lett. **54**(5), 4609–4646 (2022)
14. Gisselbaek, M., et al.: Representation of intensivists' race/ethnicity, sex, and age by artificial intelligence: a cross-sectional study of two text-to-image models. Crit. Care **28**(1), 363 (2024)
15. Goparaju, N.: Picture this: text-to-image models transforming pediatric emergency medicine. Ann. Emerg. Med. **84**(6), 651–657 (2024)

16. Gustafson, L., et al.: Facet: fairness in computer vision evaluation benchmark. In: Proceedings of the IEEE/CVF International Conference on Computer Vision, pp. 20370–20382 (2023)
17. Ho, J.Q., Hartanto, A., Koh, A., Majeed, N.M.: Gender biases within artificial intelligence and chatgpt: evidence, sources of biases and solutions. Comput. Hum. Behav. Artif. Hum. 100145 (2025)
18. Huang, L.T.L., Huang, T.R.: Generative bias: widespread, unexpected, and uninterpretable biases in generative models and their implications. AI Soc. 1–13 (2025)
19. Huang, Z., Sheng, Z., Ma, C., Chen, S.: Human as AI mentor: enhanced human-in-the-loop reinforcement learning for safe and efficient autonomous driving. Commun. Transp. Res. **4**, 100127 (2024)
20. Jiang, J., Manoranjan, V., Salam, H., Celiktutan, O.: Generalised bias mitigation for personality computing. In: Proceedings of the 1st International Workshop on Multimodal and Responsible Affective Computing, pp. 39–50 (2023)
21. Jiang, J., Manoranjan, V., Salam, H., Celiktutan, O.: Towards generalised and incremental bias mitigation in personality computing. IEEE Trans. Affect. Comput. **15**(4), 2192–2203 (2024)
22. Karkkainen, K., Joo, J.: Fairface: face attribute dataset for balanced race, gender, and age for bias measurement and mitigation. In: Proceedings of the IEEE/CVF Winter Conference on Applications of Computer Vision, pp. 1548–1558 (2021)
23. Ko, H.K., Park, G., Jeon, H., Jo, J., Kim, J., Seo, J.: Large-scale text-to-image generation models for visual artists' creative works. In: Proceedings of the 28th International Conference on Intelligent User Interfaces, pp. 919–933 (2023)
24. Labs, B.F.: Flux. 1 kontext: flow matching for in-context image generation and editing in latent space. arXiv preprint arXiv:2506.15742 (2025)
25. Lin, S., Wang, A., Yang, X.: SDXL-lightning: progressive adversarial diffusion distillation. arXiv preprint arXiv:2402.13929 (2024)
26. Liu, Y.L., et al.: Human-centered evaluation and auditing of language models. In: Proceedings of the Extended Abstracts of the CHI Conference on Human Factors in Computing Systems, pp. 1–7 (2025)
27. Luccioni, S., Akiki, C., Mitchell, M., Jernite, Y.: Stable bias: evaluating societal representations in diffusion models. Adv. Neural. Inf. Process. Syst. **36**, 56338–56351 (2023)
28. Naik, R., Nushi, B.: Social biases through the text-to-image generation lens. In: Proceedings of the 2023 AAAI/ACM Conference on AI, Ethics, and Society, pp. 786–808 (2023)
29. Olmos, C.L., Neophytou, A., Sengupta, S., Papadopoulos, D.P.: Latent directions: a simple pathway to bias mitigation in generative AI. In: Proceedings of the IEEE/CVF Conference on Computer Vision and Pattern Recognition, pp. 8333–8337 (2024)
30. Ooi, K.B., Tan, G.W.H., et al.: The potential of generative artificial intelligence across disciplines: perspectives and future directions. J. Comput. Inf. Syst. **65**(1), 76–107 (2025)
31. Podell, D., et al.: SDXL: improving latent diffusion models for high-resolution image synthesis. arXiv preprint arXiv:2307.01952 (2023)
32. Ramaswamy, V.V., Kim, S.S., Russakovsky, O.: Fair attribute classification through latent space de-biasing. In: Proceedings of the IEEE/CVF Conference on Computer Vision and Pattern Recognition, pp. 9301–9310 (2021)
33. Ramesh, A., Dhariwal, P., Nichol, A., Chu, C., Chen, M.: Hierarchical text-conditional image generation with clip latents. arXiv preprint arXiv:2204.06125 **1**(2), 3 (2022)

34. Rombach, R., Blattmann, A., Lorenz, D., Esser, P., Ommer, B.: High-resolution image synthesis with latent diffusion models. In: Proceedings of the IEEE/CVF Conference on Computer Vision and Pattern Recognition, pp. 10684–10695 (2022)
35. Saharia, C., Chan, W., et al.: Photorealistic text-to-image diffusion models with deep language understanding. Adv. Neural. Inf. Process. Syst. **35**, 36479–36494 (2022)
36. Samuel, D., Ben-Ari, R., Darshan, N., Maron, H., Chechik, G.: Norm-guided latent space exploration for text-to-image generation. Adv. Neural. Inf. Process. Syst. **36**, 57863–57875 (2023)
37. Schuhmann, C., Beaumont, R., et al.: Laion-5b: an open large-scale dataset for training next generation image-text models. Adv. Neural. Inf. Process. Syst. **35**, 25278–25294 (2022)
38. Srinivasan, K., Raman, K., Chen, J., Bendersky, M., Najork, M.: Wit: Wikipedia-based image text dataset for multimodal multilingual machine learning. In: Proceedings of the 44th International ACM SIGIR Conference on Research and Development in Information Retrieval, pp. 2443–2449 (2021)
39. Sufian, A., Ghosh, A., Barman, D., Leo, M., Distante, C.: Demobias: an empirical study to trace demographic biases in vision foundation models. In: 2025 13th International Workshop on Biometrics and Forensics (IWBF), pp. 01–06 (2025)
40. Vice, J., Akhtar, N., Hartley, R., Mian, A.: Exploring bias in over 100 text-to-image generative models. arXiv preprint arXiv:2503.08012 (2025)
41. Vice, J., Akhtar, N., Hartley, R., Mian, A.: Quantifying bias in text-to-image generative models. IEEE Trans. Dependable Secure Comput. (2025)
42. Vladimir, A., Vasilev, V., et al.: Kandinsky 3: text-to-image synthesis for multifunctional generative framework. In: Proceedings of the 2024 Conference on Empirical Methods in Natural Language Processing: System Demonstrations, pp. 475–485 (2024)
43. Wan, Y., et al.: Survey of bias in text-to-image generation: definition, evaluation, and mitigation. arXiv preprint arXiv:2404.01030 (2024)
44. Wang, W., et al.: New job, new gender? Measuring the social bias in image generation models. In: Proceedings of the 32nd ACM International Conference on Multimedia, pp. 3781–3789 (2024)
45. Wu, C., Li, J., et al.: Qwen-image technical report. arXiv preprint arXiv:2508.02324 (2025)
46. Wu, X., Xiao, L., Sun, Y., Zhang, J., Ma, T., He, L.: A survey of human-in-the-loop for machine learning. Futur. Gener. Comput. Syst. **135**, 364–381 (2022)

AΦ—Artificial Phronēsis

Rolf Hvidtfeldt[1(✉)], Mohammad N. S. Jahromi[2], and Anders Skaarup Johansen[2]

[1] Aalborg University, SSH, Copenhagen, Denmark
rolfh@hum.aau.dk
[2] Aalborg University, TECH, Aalborg, Denmark
{mosa,asjo}@create.aau.dk

Abstract. This paper examines the ethical and conceptual challenges of designing artificial intelligence systems endowed with phronetic capacities, here denoted as AΦ. By means of a minimal two-layer architecture, we contrast a low-arousal "System 1," which is minimally intrusive, compliant with regulation, and readily contestable, with a high-arousal "System 2," which offers greater life-saving potential but depends upon sensitive and arguably unlawful surveillance practices. The layered model highlights unresolved issues of proportionality, normalization of exceptional measures, asymmetry of rights across layers, and the tension between the demand for narrative continuity and the legal imperative of data minimization. Further, this configuration brings to light the contestation paradox: the very act of contesting a decision transforms anonymous data into personal data, thereby reshaping the ethical and legal conditions it is intended to protect. We contend that contestation cannot be regarded as an external safeguard but must be understood as a process that alters accountability, transparency, and privacy. We conclude that if AI systems are ever to approximate phronetic judgment, they must adapt contestation mechanisms to context, urgency, and risk. Yet this also risks granting AI the capacity to override its own rules—raising the question of whether such systems could remain both intelligent and legitimate.

Keywords: AI · Surveillance Systems · AI Arousal · AΦ · phronēsis

1 Introduction

In this paper, we introduce a hypothetical two-layered AI surveillance system designed to prevent drowning accidents at a harbor front in Aalborg, Denmark—a site where intoxicated partygoers sometimes fall into the water unnoticed. We present this hypothetical system not as an implementable specification, but as a minimal conceptual model to prompt reflection on what we call *phronetic AI* (or *AΦ*)[1], including what it would mean for AI systems to count as truly intelligent.

[1] To be clear, in this context we use "AΦ" to denote artificial intelligence systems that incorporate phronetic capacities. Part of this decision is guided by the conceptual, aesthetic, and auditive appeal of "AΦ" as a marker. One could, of course, focus specifically on artificial phronesis itself, but that is not the topic of this paper.

K. Nasrollahi et al. (Eds.): REPAI-W 2025, LNCS 16390, pp. 72–84, 2026.
https://doi.org/10.1007/978-3-032-16886-3_5

We develop this philosophical claim through technical analysis of what such a minimal two-layered AI surveillance system would require. The first layer, or low-arousal mode, performs minimal risk assessment: thermal cameras detect human presence within five meters of the harbor edge, focusing on high-risk contexts such as weekend nights. If conditions suggest potential danger, a high-arousal mode is activated. In this second layer, high-resolution imagery is used to assess intoxication and evaluate imminent risk. If an accident appears likely, the system can automatically notify rescue personnel. Should a fall occur, the high-resolution data could also support rapid identification of the victim—indeed, in case of an accident, identification is a feature rather than a flaw. We contend that a well-functioning high-arousal system of this kind is technically feasible, but likely in violation of both national and international regulations.

From an ethical perspective, questions raised by arousal systems are hardly new. Related issues have literally been debated for millennia. In the *Nicomachean Ethics*, Aristotle highlights the need to sometimes make exceptions to the law in order to act rightly in particular situations [3, V.10]. He introduces the concept (epieikeia, "equity") as a correction of legal justice, since laws are universal while life's circumstances are particular. Universal rules sometimes misfire, and certain situations cannot be clearly determined to fall within or outside the law. Other situations may be clearly illegal, yet still call for exceptions. In such cases, equitable judgment is required:

> "What creates the problem is that the equitable is just, but not the legally just but a correction of legal justice. The reason is that all law is universal but about some things it is not possible to make a universal statement which shall be correct."

Aristotle explicitly links this corrective role of equity to the concept ό (phronēsis, "practical wisdom"), the virtue that enables a person to discern the proper course of action in particular circumstances when strict application of universal law might miss the mark [3, VI.7]. In other words, equity is the practical expression of phronēsis in the domain of justice.

This Aristotelian perspective is directly relevant to AI: a system limited to rigid rule-following may calculate efficiently, but without the capacity for equity and phronēsis it cannot be considered truly intelligent—at least not if we accept Aristotle's claim that phronēsis is inseparable from full virtue and integral to being a truly good (and thus fully intelligent) human being [3, VI.13].

2 Technical Outline of a Low and High Arousal AI System

In what follows, we outline the technical requirements for a two-layer system, focusing on training data, operational thresholds, and activation criteria. This minimal model is not meant as a practical specification, but as a primitive phronetic-by-design prototype—one that, despite its simplicity, raises a range of important ethical questions.

The two-layer surveillance architecture thus represents a technical attempt to balance competing demands of public safety and individual privacy. Examining the requirements and constraints of each layer highlights fundamental tensions that arise when systems are designed to embody different ethical stances while pursuing shared operational goals. Our analysis draws on the existing thermal imaging system at Aalborg's harbor front, which provides concrete technical grounding for these reflections.

2.1 System 1: Low-Arousal

System 1 embodies the principle of privacy by design through deliberate technical constraints. The system operates continuously using thermal cameras installed at the Aalborg harbor front, processing imagery from a thermal camera that captures the harbor area in the long-wavelength infrared spectrum between 8 and 14 μm. This spectral range detects heat emissions from human bodies while remaining insensitive to visible light conditions, enabling twenty-four hour operation regardless of lighting or weather conditions.

The technical specifications of System 1 were carefully chosen to ensure GDPR compliance through technical impossibility of identification. At 288 by 384 pixel resolution with 8-bit grayscale depth, the thermal images contain insufficient information for facial recognition, gait analysis, or any other biometric identification. This is not merely a policy choice but a fundamental limitation of the physics involved. The Point Spread Function of thermal imaging at distances exceeding five meters creates natural anonymization that cannot be reversed through computational enhancement. Even advanced super-resolution techniques are incapable of recovering the amount of information necessary for biometric identification.

The training data for System 1 comprises the Long-Term Thermal-Imaging Drift dataset, an extensive collection of 1,069,428 thermal images captured over 188 days from May 2020 to April 2021. This temporal span is crucial for system robustness, as it encompasses seasonal variations with varying ambient temperatures, weather conditions, and human activity. The dataset captures the full daily cycle of harbor activity, from the quiet pre-dawn hours when individual detection is most critical to the busy afternoon periods when the system must distinguish between legitimate harbor users and potential risk scenarios.

Professional annotators meticulously labeled each frame with bounding boxes indicating human presence, following a rigorous quality control process.

The performance characteristics of System 1 reveal an interesting asymmetry that has profound implications for escalation logic. The system achieves 93.82% precision and 96.86% recall for human detection, indicating strong capability to identify when humans are present. However, for the non-human class, precision drops to 89.02% with recall at 79.92%. This asymmetric performance creates what we term a "safety bias" where the system is more likely to generate false positives, incorrectly detecting humans when none are present, than false negatives that might miss actual humans near the water.

From our confusion matrix analysis based on the sample of 62,820 test images, we observed 3,043 false positives where the system detected humans in scenes containing only environmental heat sources such as ventilation exhausts, sun-warmed surfaces, or vehicular heat signatures. These false positives represent more than mere technical errors; they constitute potential triggers for System 2 activation, each one a moment where the system must decide whether to escalate its surveillance intensity. Despite a high technical performance, it reveals a philosophical problem, namely that system failures could trigger surveillance escalations resulting in undue recordings of personally identifiable information without a substantive cause, which could lead to potential legal or ethical infractions.

2.2 System 2: High-Arousal

System 2 represents a speculative but technically feasible escalation layer that would fundamentally alter the ethical and legal status of the surveillance system. While not implemented in the current deployment, outlining its technical requirements helps illuminate the tensions inherent in adaptive surveillance architectures. Whereas System 1 is limited to inputs from the thermal sensor, System 2 could access the full sensor array of the installation, making it possible to augment the purpose and performance of System 1 with additional signals, including those enabling biometric identification. In this way, System 2 could function both as a complementary component to System 1 and as a parallel system. The integration of additional sensors would allow for more precise recognition of high-risk situations, improved prediction of incidents, and faster, more accurate alerts to the appropriate authorities.

Even if System 2 were to activate only under specific high-risk conditions—such as when System 1 detects one to three individuals near the water's edge during high-risk hours—minor inaccuracies in System 1's performance could result in significant encroachments on harbor-goers' rights to privacy. This risk is heightened by the duality of human intervention: during densely populated moments, witnesses are often present and able to intervene in emergencies, thereby reducing the need for escalated surveillance. Yet even in low-risk scenarios, escalation could lead to unwarranted intrusions into the privacy of "safe" individuals. Indeed, beyond the individuals directly detected, escalation entails collateral privacy infringements: once System 2 is activated, all bystanders in the vicinity are swept into its expanded data collection, regardless of their involvement. This means that a single misclassification does not only affect one individual but can impose disproportionate intrusions on many, raising questions of proportionality and justifiability.

Consequently, the phronetic component that determines escalation would need to be acutely sensitive to contextual and circumstantial signals that fundamentally shape whether escalation is necessary. Moreover, the very premises and rules that the phronetic component implicitly or explicitly follows raise further concerns about the functional and ethical adequacy of those rules.

Finally, any audit or contestation of such a system would require System 2 to record and retain detailed logs of all escalations. At the same time, it would be unable to document cases where escalation was warranted but dismissed—unless escalated data were continuously recorded as evidence. This creates an additional tension between accountability and privacy, further complicating the legitimacy of such an architecture.

Legally, System 2 collides with several layers of regulation. Under the GDPR, subjects have a right to restrict processing (Art. 18), to object to data collection (Art. 21), and not to be subjected to decisions based solely on automated processing (Art. 22). These rights are difficult to exercise once data are captured through opaque, cross-linked sensors. At the same time, transparency, minimization, and storage limitation—core principles of the GDPR—are strained by the very logging requirements needed for auditability. Parallel frameworks also apply: the NIS2 directive governs the cybersecurity of such installations and transmissions, while the AI Act obliges developers to ensure both transparency (Art. 13) and meaningful human oversight (Art. 14). Reduced explainability and automatic escalation therefore risk not only ethical overreach but regulatory non-compliance.

3 Related Work

As sketched out above, from the Aristotelian perspective, an intelligent system cannot be considered truly intelligent if it merely applies fixed rules or statistical correlations. Genuine intelligence requires the capacity for phronēsis—the situational discernment that knows when and how rules must bend to context. Without such capacities, AI risks reducing decision-making to mechanical calculation. Current AI ethics frameworks, centered on fairness, accountability, and transparency (FAT), rightly stress consistency and procedural safeguards, but they stop short of addressing this deeper demand. As Aristotle reminds us, genuine justice also requires situational discernment—judgment in legal grey areas and responsiveness to particular contexts. An AI system built only on rules and metrics cannot satisfy this requirement.

While no existing AI system, to our knowledge, embodies such phronetic capacities, adjacent strands of research in governance, exception recognition, and hybrid architectures offer partial scaffolding—resources that can help us imagine what "phronesis by design" might require.

The balance between competing accountability policies remains "a matter of ongoing ethical deliberation" [5]. Current privacy-preserving technologies are insufficient for complex accountability requirements, and regulatory frameworks continue to lag behind both technical capabilities and ethical demands. Recent scholarship has begun to challenge the assumption that abstract, universal principles can adequately guide AI accountability. Mager [8], for instance, argues that ostensibly universal concepts such as privacy and accountability take on context-specific meanings shaped by cultural and situational factors. This line of work directly supports the need for AI systems whose ethical constraints vary with context—an approach resonant with our notion of arousal-sensitive governance.

Parallel work examines AI under crisis conditions. Visave et al. [17] propose governance protocols where AI operating in emergencies may legitimately suspend or alter normal regulatory frameworks. Their findings identify a critical gap between standard AI governance models and the requirements of rapid, high-stakes decision-making—precisely the type of tension illustrated by our harbor surveillance case.

A growing body of literature also emphasizes that accountability and contestability cannot be treated as static, one-off guarantees but must evolve dynamically across time and contexts. Noorman et al. [9] highlight governance models that adapt to shifting operational conditions, while De et al. [4] show how algorithmic recourse recommendations degrade as contexts change, coining the notion of *temporal invalidation.* To counter this, methods for "temporal algorithmic recourse" explicitly model contextual evolution. Similarly, Alfrink et al. [1] introduce *contestability loops*, whereby challenges and appeals occur continuously throughout a system's lifecycle rather than at isolated checkpoints. Pareek et al. [12] further stress that trust in AI systems is dynamic and shaped by temporal factors such as stakes and outcomes. Collectively, these contributions push contestability from static, design-time features toward adaptive, runtime processes—though important gaps remain in mechanisms that recalibrate contestation under evolving operational conditions.

While no paper delivers a full-stack, surveillance-specific system embodying "phronesis by design," several strands provide partial scaffolding. For instance, proportionality-based governance methods decompose risk and balance competing values through scenario-specific thresholds, offering case-sensitive justifications aligned with doctrines such as necessity and proportionality [10, 11]. Second, legal-logic approaches integrate proportionality with defeasible reasoning, yielding structured, auditable arguments even under vague or conflicting norms [2, 14]. Third, exception recognition can be benchmarked using datasets like RBQA, enabling evaluation of whether departures from defaults align with human judgment in difficult cases [7]. Fourth, hybrid moral architectures combine learned perception with symbolic deliberation layers and runtime monitors, promising both adaptability and control under uncertainty [15]. Fifth, imitation-based approaches, such as knowledge distillation and student–teacher learning, move away from strict metric optimization and instead aim to align behavior with a distribution of candidate responses, often grounded in human examples. While still firmly within the domain of mathematical modeling, such paradigms approximate a pseudo-phronetic system: they accept sub-optimal or varied short-term outputs in order to capture longer-term patterns of judgment, using softer, more lenient targets than conventional optimization allows [18].

Taken together, these strands converge on several principles that a phronetic surveillance system would require: proportionality tests, defeasible reasoning, human-auditable explanations, and hybrid architectures with graded autonomy and escalation. Yet notable absences remain: no runtime "break-glass" handlers with explicit proportionality triggers; no evaluation artifacts for exception quality, near-miss learning, or rights-impact stratification; and no HCI mechanisms such as operator decision aids or contestation channels integrated with reason logs [7,10,11]. Though conditional decision-making and imitation learning might superficially resemble phronetic judgment—by training systems to imitate human auditors or align with prior cases—they remain statistical approximations of contextual response rather than genuine practical wisdom. In computer science, such situations are often described as "ill-posed problems," since the optimization path itself becomes ambiguous once the objective extends beyond measurable metrics. Current solutions tend to rely on global approximators, which, as discussed above, are precisely what prove insufficient in legal, ethical, and societal contexts. This tension highlights the deep mismatch between the aims of machine learning and the requirements of phronetic judgment.

From an ethical perspective, this reinforces the gap. Existing approaches scaffold fairness, accountability, and transparency, but they stop short of addressing phronēsis—the capacity for judgment that can suspend or reinterpret universal rules in light of particular circumstances. In an AI Arousal system such as our harbor example, this would mean not only detecting intoxicated individuals or triggering alarms, but reasoning about when proportionality justifies invasive measures, when escalation is warranted, and how reasons for such decisions should be logged and contestable. Without such capacities, AI systems may calculate, but they cannot judge—and thus cannot be considered intelligent in the full Aristotelian sense.

4 Ethical Considerations and The Contestation Paradox

The ethical dilemma is clear. On one hand, System 1 is minimally intrusive, GDPR-compliant, and functions only as a gatekeeper. It does little harm, but it also does little to prevent actual accidents. On the other hand, System 2 could save lives, but only by mobilizing deeply sensitive and arguably unlawful surveillance practices. If activated solely in narrowly defined, high-risk scenarios, does this two-layer structure represent a reasonable trade-off between privacy and safety? Or does it risk normalizing extreme surveillance under the guise of proportionality? Figure 1 illustrates how this apparent binary choice between between the two systems unfolds as a multidimensional, asymmetric normative tension. Even when high-intrusion measures are intended to remain exceptional, institutional inertia and bureaucratic expansion can gradually normalize them, transforming rare exceptions into standard practice.

One way to think about this is by analogy. In high-stakes situations, we often permit actions that would otherwise violate important principles: violence may be justified in self-defence, breaking a car window is excusable if it saves a child from heatstroke, and doctors may act without consent in medical emergencies. In such cases, the suspension of principles is justified by urgency and proportionality, guided by situational judgment. Unlike traditional emergency exceptions, where proportionality is often clear—violence is limited to what is necessary for self-defence—surveillance interventions lack such obvious boundaries, making proportionality judgments in AI inherently more complex .

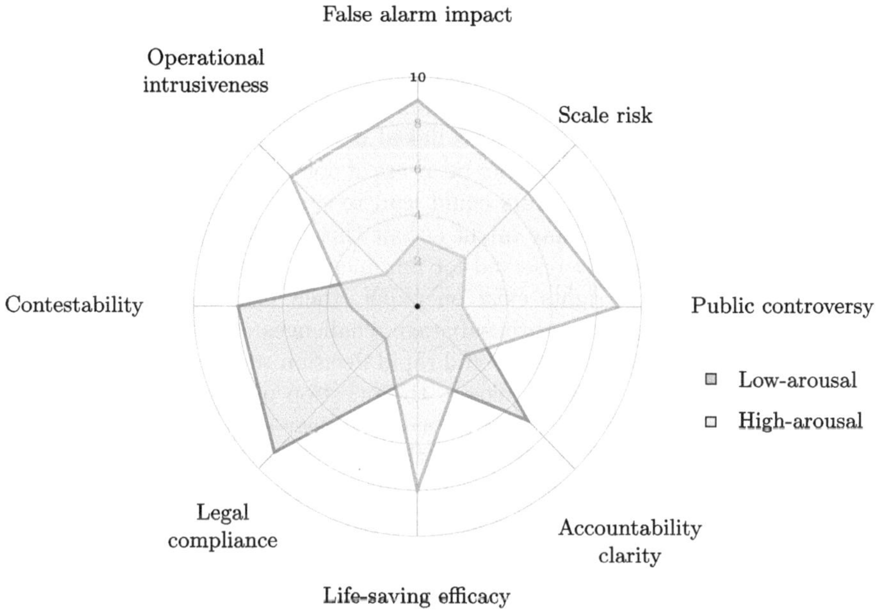

Fig. 1. Radar chart comparing low- and high-arousal layers on 8 dimensions (0–10 scale) with green=mostly goodand red=mostly bad. **Contestability**: How easy is it to challenge a decision? **Legal compliance**: Does it stay within regulatory boundaries? **Life-saving efficacy**: Contribution to preventing drowning? **Accountability clarity**: Clear responsibility if something goes wrong? **Scale risk**: How easily could this model spread beyond harbors into other areas of life? **Public controversy**: How much resistance or distrust will the system provoke? **False alarm impact**: Privacy infringements caused by false alarms. **Operational intrusiveness**: Depth of system intervention in private life. The high-arousal layer is clearly worse than the low-arousal layer except for its ability to save lives. (Color figure online)

Yet this analogy also points to a deeper concern. Acts of self-defence or breaking a window remain exceptional. Once institutionalized, however, surveillance systems risk becoming precedents. Does the layered design protect us by ensuring that high-intrusion measures remain rare and exceptional? Or does it instead carve out a pathway for normalizing invasive surveillance under the banner of proportionality? A further and more difficult question concerns what would happen if the ability to override rules more generally were built into AI systems. If we do not want this capacity in its simplest form, we certainly cannot permit it in more general settings. Yet refusing it altogether may mean abandoning the possibility of ever developing AGI (or, perhaps, AGΦ?).

4.1 The Contestation Paradox

Another dimension concerns contestation. In a purely low-arousal system, decisions are relatively transparent and easily contestable: individuals can request to see the data, understand the rules applied, and challenge errors, since the system works only with low-resolution, non-sensitive information. This transparency helps maintain trust and democratic legitimacy. By contrast, once the high-arousal system is activated, contestability becomes far more difficult. The system would draw on sensitive, cross-linked datasets and complex behavioral analyses that individuals may neither be aware of nor able to challenge effectively. Here, the stakes are higher: errors could lead to serious intrusions or stigmatization. Yet paradoxically, many might accept this reduced contestability if the high-arousal state is strictly reserved for imminent life-and-death scenarios.

Even if contestation rights exist on paper, their effectiveness differs radically across layers. In the low-arousal stage, challenges are feasible, but in the high-arousal stage, opaque datasets and rapid decision-making render rights difficult to exercise in practice. Moreover, the question of who sets and oversees the thresholds for escalation is critical: without clear accountability, these systems concentrate power in the hands of those defining the criteria, potentially exacerbating biases and undermining legitimacy.

The act of contestation itself also transforms the nature of the data. Our thermal imaging system initially processes low-resolution, arguably non-personal data under GDPR. However, when someone contests a decision, they necessarily identify themselves as the subject of a specific detection event. This creates what we might call a contestation paradox: the very mechanism designed to protect rights converts anonymous data into personal data. The paradox reveals a deeper philosophical tension. Phronesis requires narrative continuity—understanding how situations develop over time. Privacy-preserving systems, however, must forget, treating each moment in isolation. Thus the very mechanisms intended to ensure accountability (contestation) and to protect rights (privacy) obstruct the temporal reasoning essential to phronetic judgment. Such negative privacy impacts of contestation remain largely overlooked in existing research on AI contestability, e.g., [6,13,16].

Most regulatory and ethical guidelines treat AI decisions as discrete, unitary events: an algorithm produces an output, and individuals have a right to contest it. But in layered architectures, decision-making unfolds across escalating states of arousal. The first layer may be fully transparent, rule-based, and easily challenged. The second is triggered only under heightened risk and may rely on opaque, sensitive, and highly integrated datasets.

This raises two unresolved questions. First, how should rights to contestation be distributed across layers? Is transparency at the low-arousal stage sufficient to legitimize opacity at the high-arousal stage? Second, what mechanisms can ensure that the criteria for escalation from one layer to another are themselves contestable? If the gateway from low to high arousal is flawed or biased, the entire system risks sliding into overreach while still appearing compliant.

In short, layered systems stretch existing accountability frameworks beyond their current design. They expose a blind spot: how to regulate not only individual decisions, but also the escalation between decision-making regimes. Even if one were to imagine a less radical "aroused layer," the fundamental questions would remain.

5 Discussion

Even if we imagine a traditional one-layer surveillance system, the problem of contestation does not disappear. The very act of challenging a decision transforms the nature of the data being processed: what begins as anonymous, low-resolution thermal information becomes personal data the moment an individual identifies themselves as the subject of a detection event. This contestation paradox shows that accountability mechanisms cannot be treated as neutral add-ons to technical infrastructures. They reshape the ethical and legal status of the data they touch.

This observation suggests that contestation is not merely a procedural safeguard layered on top of decision-making systems. Rather, it is constitutive: once in play, it redefines what the system is and how it operates. Existing accountability frameworks, designed around the assumption that decisions are discrete, self-contained events, do not adequately capture this dynamic. In layered or temporally extended systems, contestation becomes part of the very architecture of decision-making, fundamentally altering its ethical landscape.

The harbor-front case illustrates a further challenge: contestation does not have the same meaning in all contexts. A detection at 3 PM during business hours carries very different ethical and practical implications from a detection at 3 AM near the water's edge. In the first case, the stakes are low, time is available for appeal, and individuals can reasonably expect due process. In the second, immediacy and danger require rapid escalation, even at the expense of reduced transparency.

This temporal and contextual variation reveals the limitations of static contestation frameworks. If contestation mechanisms are rigid and uniform, they will either be too slow to preserve life in emergencies or too weak to preserve rights in ordinary contexts. A more promising approach would be to recognize contestation as adaptive: its procedures and intensity must scale with the urgency and risk level of the decision at hand. The key research question becomes: how should contestation rights and mechanisms adapt to the temporal stakes of AI decisions?

Taken together, these reflections reopen the question of what it might mean to design phronetic AI. If contestation is inherently transformative, and if its proper form varies with urgency and risk, then any adequate system must be capable of modifying not only its decisions but also its modes of accountability in response to circumstances. In effect, this would require building systems that exercise something like judgment: the ability to deviate from rigid procedural rules when proportionality and context demand it.

This possibility is both tempting and troubling. On one hand, the ability to override fixed rules in light of context might be essential to the development of truly intelligent systems. On the other, deliberately constructing AI with such override capacities risks undermining the very structures of legality and accountability that make its operation legitimate. One could argue that this tension marks the frontier of artificial general intelligence: if intelligence requires phronesis, then it also requires the possibility of exception. The challenge, then, is ensuring that such judgment is not merely functional, but virtuous—aligned with the best possible standards of human practical wisdom.

Aristotle taught that phronesis entails discerning how universal rules must bend in the face of particular circumstances. Contestation, as we have argued, is inherently dynamic: it alters the meaning of data, shifts the ethical terrain, and demands adaptation to temporal stakes. If AI systems are ever to count as phronetic, they must be designed to engage with such dynamic adaptations rather than deny or suppress them. Yet doing so risks crossing the threshold into AI with the capacity to override its own rules—including, crucially, the very rules for contestation—leaving open whether such systems could ever be both intelligent and legitimate.

5.1 Issues for Further Debate

These reflections raise several questions for future debate. First, to what extent can "exceptional" surveillance practices remain genuinely bounded, or will institutional inertia and bureaucratic expansion make them spread once institutionalized? Second, what principles should govern the adaptation of contestation rights to different levels of urgency and risk—and must such principles themselves remain flexible, in the Aristotelian sense of equity? Third, how can systems reconcile the demand for narrative continuity, necessary for phronetic judgment, with GDPR's emphasis on data minimization and forgetting? Fourth and finally, is the capacity to override operational rules truly a necessary step toward AGI—and if so, how might such capacity be disciplined so that judgment remains virtuous rather than dangerous?

These questions invite further research and debate. They also demonstrate the value of combining speculative technical modelling with philosophical reflection on real-world cases and problems. In particular, future work must attend to the limits of delegation: even a phronetic system trained on today's norms may drift out of alignment as societal values evolve, risking normalization of excessive surveillance. This underscores the enduring need for meaningful human oversight—whether in real time or through post-hoc review—as a safeguard of accountability and legitimacy.

6 Conclusion

In closing, our minimal model was never intended as an implementable system, but as a probe into the possibility of phronetic AI. The contestation paradox shows that even simple architectures reveal deep tensions between intelligence, judgment, and legitimacy. Designing AI capable of phronetic judgment requires grappling with the transformative effects of contestation and the need to adapt to temporal and contextual stakes. But phronesis presupposes narrative continuity, while GDPR enforces forgetting; in this sense, European privacy law may make AΦ legally impossible, not just technically difficult. Similarly, optimization in machine learning requires fixed, measurable targets, whereas ethical and legal judgment demands contextual, open-ended reasoning. This tension—an ill-posed optimization problem—suggests that any attempt to build AΦ will collide with the very structures meant to ensure accountability. If so, the very capacities that suggest intelligence could simultaneously place these systems beyond democratic acceptability. More provocatively, if AΦ is impossible or undesirable, then pursuing artificial general intelligence in the first place may be ethically indefensible—we should reconsider chasing AGI unless we are willing to commit to systems capable of virtuous, rule-bending judgment.

Acknowledgments. This research is supported by the Grundfos Foundation ("REPAI", grant no. 83648813) and Independent Research Fund Denmark ("Contestable Artificial Intelligence", grant no. 10.46540/2027-00140B).

References

1. Alfrink, K., Keller, I., Semperena, M.Y., Bulygin, D., Kortuem, G., Doorn, N.: Envisioning contestability loops: evaluating the agonistic arena as a generative metaphor for public AI. She Ji J. Des. Econ. Innov. **10**(1), 53–93 (2024)
2. Arias, J., Moreno-Rebato, M., Rodriguez-Garcia, J.A., Ossowski, S.: Towards value-awareness in administrative processes: an approach based on constraint answer set programming. In: Proceedings of the 39th ACM/SIGAPP Symposium on Applied Computing, pp. 770–778 (2024)
3. Aristotle: Nicomachean Ethics. Hackett, Indianapolis, 2nd edn. (1999)
4. De Toni, G., Teso, S., Lepri, B., Passerini, A.: Time can invalidate algorithmic recourse. In: Proceedings of the 2025 ACM Conference on Fairness, Accountability, and Transparency, pp. 89–107 (2025)
5. Floridi, L.: The ethics of artificial intelligence: principles, challenges, and opportunities (2023)
6. Hirsch, T., Merced, K., Narayanan, S., Imel, Z.E., Atkins, D.C.: Designing contestability: interaction design, machine learning, and mental health. In: Proceedings of the 2017 Conference on Designing Interactive Systems, pp. 95–99 (2017)
7. Jin, Z., et al.: When to make exceptions: exploring language models as accounts of human moral judgment (2022). https://arxiv.org/abs/2210.01478
8. Mager, A., Eitenberger, M., Winter, J., Prainsack, B., Wendehorst, C., Arora, P.: Situated ethics: ethical accountability of local perspectives in global AI ethics. Media Cult. Soc. **47**(5), 1028–1041 (2025)
9. Noorman, M.: The governance of AI technologies. In: Computer Ethics Across Disciplines: Deborah G. Johnson and Algorithmic Accountability, pp. 85–102. Springer (2025)
10. Novelli, C., Casolari, F., Rotolo, A., Taddeo, M., Floridi, L.: How to evaluate the risks of artificial intelligence: a proportionality-based, risk model for the AI act. SSRN Electron. J. (2023)

11. Novelli, C., Casolari, F., Rotolo, A., Taddeo, M., Floridi, L.: Ai risk assessment: a scenario-based, proportional methodology for the AI act. Digit. Soc. **3**(1), 13 (2024)
12. Pareek, S., Schömbs, S., Velloso, E., Goncalves, J.: "It's not the AI's fault because it relies purely on data": how causal attributions of AI decisions shape trust in AI systems. In: Proceedings of the 2025 CHI Conference on Human Factors in Computing Systems, pp. 1–18 (2025)
13. Ploug, T., Holm, S.: The four dimensions of contestable AI diagnostics-a patient-centric approach to explainable AI. Artif. Intell. Med. **107**, 101901 (2020)
14. Rotolo, A., Ferrigno, B., Godinez, J.M.A.G., Novelli, C., Sartor, G.: Foundations for risk assessment of AI in protecting fundamental rights (2025). https://arxiv.org/abs/2507.18290
15. Tennant, E., Hailes, S., Musolesi, M.: Hybrid approaches for moral value alignment in AI agents: a manifesto (2025). https://arxiv.org/abs/2312.01818
16. Vaccaro, K., Karahalios, K., Mulligan, D.K., Kluttz, D., Hirsch, T.: Contestability in algorithmic systems. In: Companion Publication of the 2019 Conference on Computer Supported Cooperative Work and Social Computing, pp. 523–527 (2019)
17. Visave, J.: Ai in emergency management: ethical considerations and challenges. J. Emerg. Manag. Disaster Commun. **5**(01), 165–183 (2024)
18. Zare, M., Kebria, P.M., Khosravi, A., Nahavandi, S.: A survey of imitation learning: algorithms, recent developments, and challenges. IEEE Trans. Cybern. (2024)

Presenting Issues in Employee Assistance Programmes: Towards an LLM-Based Support Tool for Counsellor Support and Assistance

Gillian Cameron[1,2](✉), Maurice Mulvenna[2], Raymond Bond[2], Edel Ennis[3], Siobhan O'Neill[3], Patrick McAllister[2], and David Cameron[1]

[1] Lena (by Inspire), 1020 Lombard Street, Belfast BT1 1RD, UK
{cameron-g2,cameron-g2}@ulster.ac.uk

[2] School of Computing, Ulster University, Belfast BT15 1AP, UK

[3] School of Psychology, Ulster University, Coleraine BT52 1SA, UK

Abstract. Meaningful employment can enhance both mental and physical wellbeing, but over 15% of the global workforce shows signs of a mental health disorder. Evidence suggests that anxiety and depression, the most prevalent mental health conditions, can be successfully prevented or addressed through workplace interventions. Recent advances in machine learning and artificial intelligence have seen effective applications in the mental health sphere, from assisting in counselling conversations and topics, detecting mental health conditions, and creating mental health chatbots or conversational agents.

This study aimed to analyse and model the presenting issues, which are issues offered by a client or a patient as the reason for seeking treatment, from an Employee Assistance Programme (EAP) service. A dataset containing presenting issues at point of referral was analysed, seeking to reduce the dimensionality of these 1126 presenting issues using Latent Dirichlet Allocation (LDA), and 8 main topics were found: 1. Work-related stress and life pressures, 2. Family conflict, 3. Neurodiversity and transitions, 4. Family health and sleep, 5. Relationship breakdown and illness, 6. Suicidal Ideation, 7. Low mood and self-harm, 8. Anger and body image. Given the critical role that accurate presenting issue classification plays in triage, care planning, and service monitoring, this study first seeks to understand these unstructured entries through topic modelling and then explores how the insights gained may inform the development of AI-assisted tools to support counsellors at this early, yet essential, stage of client engagement. Through this approach, the research addressed key challenges in understanding presenting issues within an employee assistance programme, and motivates future empirical work to design an AI-enabled, data-driven counsellor support tool for classifying presenting issues within employee assistance programmes.

Keywords: Mental health · presenting issues · employee assistance programmes · large language models · topic modelling · Latent Dirichlet Allocation · machine learning · artificial intelligence

K. Nasrollahi et al. (Eds.): REPAI-W 2025, LNCS 16390, pp. 85–100, 2026.
https://doi.org/10.1007/978-3-032-16886-3_6

1 Introduction

1.1 Mental Health in the Workplace and Employee Assistance Programmes (EAPs)

Meaningful employment can enhance both mental and physical wellbeing [1], but over 15% of the global workforce shows signs of a mental health disorder [2]. In the UK alone, stress, anxiety, and depression accounted for 16.4 million lost working days in 2023–2024 [3], and each year, more than 300,000 individuals with long-term mental health conditions lose their jobs [4]. Research indicates that the most common mental health issues, anxiety and depression can be effectively prevented or managed within the workplace [5]. When left unaddressed, these conditions are associated with increased absenteeism, presenteeism, high staff turnover, diminished performance, and reduced productivity [6]. As it is estimated we spend around 84,000 h of our lives at work, it is important to maintain our wellbeing at work.

Employee Assistance Programmes (EAPs) are predominantly funded by employers and offer confidential support to employees facing personal, psychological, or work-related challenges that may impact their wellbeing or job performance. Initially developed in mid-20th century North America as a governmental initiative to address substance misuse in the workplace [7], EAPs have since expanded into comprehensive counselling and wellbeing services. Today, they are commonly delivered by external third-party providers and encompass a broader range of support mechanisms [8].

Presenting issues, which are issues given by a client or a patient as the reason for seeking treatment, can be an important factor when deciding on treatment pathways and can help to predict the number of appointments needed per case, as seen in child and adolescent mental health services in England [9]. Many studies assessing EAPs focus on utilisation, outcomes on issues such as absenteeism and presenteeism [10] or barriers to access, rather than the primary presenting issue with which an employee may enter the service. Data for this study has been obtained from Lena (by Inspire), a social enterprise operating in the United Kingdom and Ireland, that provide EAP services including counselling services. Lena have collected a large dataset of client journeys, including presenting issues at point of referral.

1.2 Machine Learning and Mental Health Data

The availability of mental health data is on the rise, but processing can be challenging due to data being unstructured, or noisy. Using techniques such as machine learning to analyse mental health data can allow researchers to estimate the effects that mental illnesses have had and will have on global populations. By identifying trends and patterns that are supported by data, this can help to drive improvements in mental health services, and potentially patient outcomes.

Machine learning approaches have been applied to predict the prevalence, factors, and effects of mental health problems (depression, social connectedness, and anxiety disorder) on college students with promising results [11]. Unsupervised machine learning techniques including association rule mining [12] and clustering [13] have been applied to user event logs produced by a workplace digital mental health intervention. A prediction modelling approach has been used on electronic health records to accurately identify patients at risk of suicide [14]. Machine learning approaches have also been used in the past to accurately predict generalised anxiety disorder in women [15].

Laricheva [16] found a growing trend of research utilising advanced machine learning methods, particularly natural language processing (NLP) techniques within counselling and psychotherapy, however there were concerns relating to bias and the generalisability of the findings. Carron-Arthur et al. [17] utilised Latent Dirichlet Allocation (LDA), an unsupervised machine learning technique method to model over 130,000 online posts within an online mental health support group, finding 21 topics within the data. LDA has been applied more recently to depression online forums, finding 13 topics, clustered into four types; medicalised, intimacy-oriented, critical and uninhabitable self-narratives [18]. Furthermore, machine learning and deep learning approaches have been utilised to diagnose mental health conditions including depression, anxiety, bipolar disorder, and post-traumatic stress disorder (PTSD) [19].

1.3 LLMs and Recommender Systems in Mental Health

LLMs and recommender systems have been applied to the context of mental health in various settings. Gunal, Lin and Bouneffouf [20] leveraged this technology to provide counselling conversation topic recommendations between patients and mental health professionals. Guo et al. [21], in a recent systematic review, found LLMs have been predominantly applied to use cases of evaluating text to detect mental health conditions and suicidal ideation, and creating mental health chatbots or conversational agents.

While LLMs show promise in providing 24/7, scalable, convenient mental health support, there are many ethical considerations and associated risks. This includes LLMs confabulating or hallucinating, in other words generating nonfactual content [22], exhibiting sycophantic behaviour, by excessively agreeing with the user or using excessive flattery [23] can erode user trust [24]. A recent tragic and extreme suicidal case in the United States linked to the use of ChatGPT further reinforces stringent safeguarding measures when implementing these types of technologies within mental health. Li et al. [25] propose the CORE (Chain of Risk Evaluation) framework to categorize and address risks in human–LLM interactions, underscoring the need for interdisciplinary safeguards in public mental health contexts.

Despite the growing application of machine learning and LLMs in mental health contexts, their use within workplace wellbeing services particularly Employee Assistance Programmes (EAPs) remains underexplored. Most existing EAP research focuses on utilisation rates, outcomes like absenteeism, or access barriers, rather than examining the qualitative content of presenting issues [10]. Furthermore, while structured taxonomies such as ICD or DSM offer consistency in clinical diagnosis, they are rarely applied in non-clinical counselling settings like EAPs, where presenting problems are often recorded in unstructured or semi-structured formats. This creates a missed opportunity for more consistent data analysis, early identification of complex cases, and improved service design. Counselling involves multiple stages, from assessment to intervention and follow-up, and this paper focuses exclusively on the early-stage task of interpreting and categorising presenting issues. This classification step, while often brief and administrative, can play a crucial role in shaping service design, resource allocation and planning. Additionally, little research has addressed how emerging AI might be responsibly integrated to support counsellors without compromising safety, ethics, or autonomy. To address these gaps, the current study investigates how topic modelling and LLMs can be used to structure and interpret presenting issues in EAP data, laying the foundation for an AI-assisted counsellor support tool.

1.4 Study Aim and Objectives

Building on these advancements and considerations, the aim of this study is to analyse and model presenting issues from an EAP service to fulfil the following objectives:

- Reduce the dimensionality of presenting problems using topic modelling;
- Explore the potential of an LLM-based support tool to assist counsellors in classifying client presenting issues and triaging cases more efficiently; and
- Present a conceptual design of an LLM-based support tool, for counsellor support with presenting issue classification and triage.

2 Methodology

This is a secondary data analysis project in which a presenting issues dataset obtained from Lena was analysed using a data analytics approach. Ulster University's Faculty of Computing, Engineering and the Built Environment ethics filter committee approved this project (CEBE_RE-24-004) and Lena has conducted a data protection impact assessment.

2.1 Dataset Summary

The dataset contains clients with a range of presenting issues that have used the Lena EAP. A total of 63,783 clients were included in the analysis. The dataset ranges from 2011 to December 2024. All genders and clients above 18 years of age were included in the analysis. In total, the dataset includes 304,485 records of presenting issues, each row containing an ID, the problem, severity and duration.

Within this, there were 1140 distinct presenting issues entered into the system by a counsellor at point of referral, some selected from a drop-down list of 14 predefined categories of presenting issue, and some entered as free text. Each client could have multiple presenting issues, with the maximum number identified as 15. All information is collected by a counsellor and inputted into a client management system.

0.62% of the dataset (n = 1893) were free text entries, and the frequency count of the predefined categories of presenting issues is displayed in Fig. 1. Of this figure, there were 1126 distinct free text entry presenting issues entered.. A subset of the data was created with these free text entries for further analysis and LDA. All analyses were conducted in R (version 4.4.2) and results are presented below.

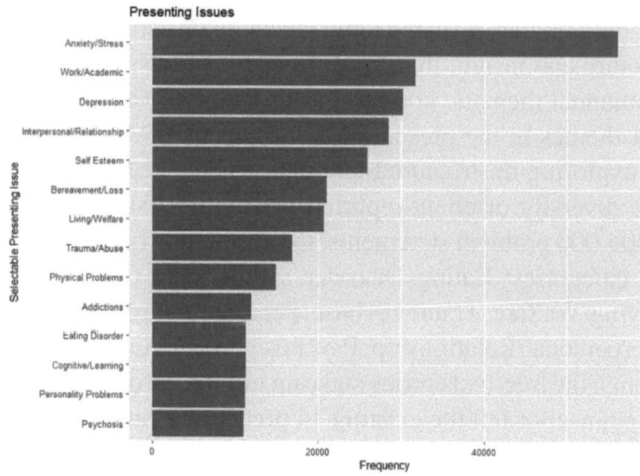

Fig. 1. Selectable pre-defined presenting issue inputs, by frequency

2.2 Preprocessing

Text preprocessing was conducted using the tm, textmineR, and dplyr packages in R (version 4.4.2). The following steps were applied to the "Problem" variable, creating a new column called "Problem_clean" to preserve the original data. All text to were changed to lowercase, along with the removal of punctuation numbers, and stop words. Common prefixes such as "Other -" were removed to reduce artificial topic inflation. This was followed by removing generic or redundant terms such as "problem", "issue", "disorder" which added little value to modelling. Any whitespace was collapsed into single spaces. Next, a text corpus was created from the cleaned text, which was converted into a Document-Term Matrix (DTM) using the tm::DocumentTermMatrix() function. Words shorter than 3 characters were excluded and stop words were removed using the default stop word list. The resulting DTM was then converted into a sparse matrix using the slam and Matrix packages for improved computational efficiency during modelling.

2.3 Latent Topic Modelling

Latent Dirichlet Allocation (LDA) is an unsupervised machine learning technique that produces a summary set of terms, to uncover hidden thematic structures (topics) within a collection of documents [26]. Topic modelling using LDA differs substantially from simpler techniques such as word frequency analysis or word clouds. While this can display the most frequently occurring terms in a dataset, they do not account for context, co-occurrence patterns, or latent themes. LDA uncovers clusters of co-occurring words that tend to appear together across documents, revealing hidden thematic structures that are not obvious from looking at the frequency of word counts. Thematic analysis involves a manual process where researchers code and group themes based on their interpretation of the data, whereas LDA offers an unsupervised and scalable approach, which is particularly well-suited to large datasets where manual coding would be impractical. Thematic analysis can have room for bias, whereas LDA relies on mathematical patterns in the data rather than researcher subjectivity, though it still requires interpretation at the point of assigning human-readable topic labels. In this study, LDA was selected as it offers more structure and insight than word frequency tools, but greater scalability and objectivity than manual thematic coding. In this study, topic modelling was employed to identify latent themes in the presenting issues using LDA. This approach is particularly useful in exploring unstructured text data where predefined categories may not fully capture the diversity of client-reported presenting issues. While the full dataset contained over 304,000 problem statements, the vast majority (99.38%) were associated with predefined categories; Eating Disorder, Addictions, Cognitive/Learning, Physical Problems, Living/Welfare, Trauma/Abuse, Personality Problems, Bereavement/Loss, Self Esteem, Interpersonal/Relationship, Psychosis, Work/Academic, Depression, Anxiety/Stress. Although the free-text entries make up just 0.62% of the dataset, they represent cases where the counsellor felt the existing 14 predefined categories did not adequately capture the client's presenting issue. These entries often reflect ambiguity, complexity, or nuanced concerns that are not easily classified. This subset therefore provides insight into unmet categorisation needs within the system and may highlight emerging or underrepresented themes.

These structured entries, while useful for categorisation, introduced significant topic dominance when included in unsupervised topic modelling, resulting in skewed outputs where a small number of predefined topics overwhelmed the model.

To better explore the thematic content within client-reported issues, the subset of free-text responses ($n = 1{,}893$; 0.62% of the dataset) that were not constrained by predefined labels were isolated and used for analysis in this study. This approach enabled the model to process free-text entries without being disproportionately influenced by the repeated structured entries. By focusing on this unstructured portion of the dataset, subtler or more complex presenting issues that may not be well represented in predefined categories may be captured, enhancing the qualitative richness and interpretability of the topic modelling output.

Topic coherence is a metric that quantifies how similar semantically the words are within a single topic, acting as a proxy for topic quality. To determine the optimal number of topics for the LDA model, topic coherence scores across multiple values of k (number of topics) were evaluated, ranging between 4 and 10. The model with 8 topics ($k = 8$) produced the highest mean coherence score.

With these considerations, and the size of the dataset, 8 was selected to ensure the topics were interpretable and meaningful. This also mitigates the risk of the model overfitting, which can occur if it becomes too complex with too many topics, leading to the extraction of noise rather than meaningful patterns. Furthermore, a more manageable number of topics ensures that the findings are practical and actionable for stakeholders, such as counsellors. Short human-readable labels were derived for each topic by concatenating the top five most probable terms.

Overall, this approach enabled the unsupervised grouping of thousands of free-text problem statements into a manageable number of semantically coherent categories, laying the groundwork for mapping to structured clinical taxonomies and designing intelligent recommendation interfaces. To our knowledge, this is the first study using EAP data to classify presenting issues using the LDA machine learning approach.

3 Results

3.1 Topic Modelling Results

Focusing on the 1126 distinct free text entries that were not captured by the predefined categories list including Anxiety/Stress, Bereavement/Loss, Depression etc., unsupervised topic modelling was conducted to uncover latent themes. LDA was applied to this subset of data using the optimal number of topics (K = 8) based on coherence score optimisation across multiple candidate values between 4 and 10 (Fig. 2).

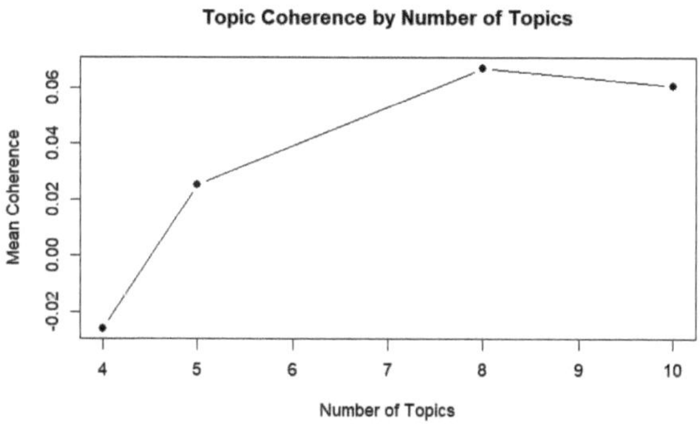

Fig. 2. Topic coherence score for models with K values ranging between 4 and 10

Top terms were extracted for each topic, and the terms are sorted by their respective weights. Suggested labels were assigned manually based on the top terms (Table 1). For example, topic 1 "Work-related stress and life pressures", which represents 46.5% of the dataset, had top ten terms of "work", "stress", "related", "life", "career", "balance", "bullying", "health", "anxiety", "trauma". While some of the topics found through LDA, such as "Work-related stress and life pressures" may appear similar to existing predefined categories, the modelling revealed some co-occurring themes. For example, Topic 1 combined work, stress, bullying, trauma, and health, highlighting the multifaceted nature of work-related distress beyond the broad "Work/Academic" label.

Table 1. Topic Modelling Summary (k = 8)

Suggested Label	Top 5 Terms (with weights)	Number of entries	Percentage of dataset %
1. Work-related stress and life pressures	work (0.1771), stress (0.0877), related (0.0466), life (0.0448), career (0.0323)	880	46.5

(continued)

Table 1. (*continued*)

Suggested Label	Top 5 Terms (with weights)	Number of entries	Percentage of dataset %
2. Family conflict	family (0.4639), financial (0.0446), underlying (0.0381), conflict (0.0368), illness (0.0354)	231	12.2
3. Neurodiversity and transitions	impact (0.1448), bullying (0.0696), transition (0.0508), adhd (0.0490), aspergers (0.0377)	172	9.1
4. Family health and sleep	family (0.1201), health (0.0741), sleep (0.0461), illness (0.0341), child (0.0241)	143	7.6
5. Relationship breakdown and illness	relationship (0.0501), work (0.0372), separation (0.0356), marital (0.0259), cancer (0.0243)	138	7.3
6. Suicidal Ideation	family (0.0344), suicidal (0.0303), ideation (0.0283), ago (0.0243), years (0.0243)	137	7.2
7. Low mood and self-harm	low (0.1069), mood (0.1017), self (0.0912), harm (0.0600), anxiety (0.0548)	117	6.2
8. Anger and body image	anger (0.1994), body (0.0500), image (0.0301), identity (0.0301), management (0.0301)	75	4

A bar plot of the topic prevalence in Fig. 3 shows 46.5% of the free-text entries fall under topic one, work-related stress and life pressures, followed by family related difficulties and then neurodiversity/transitions.

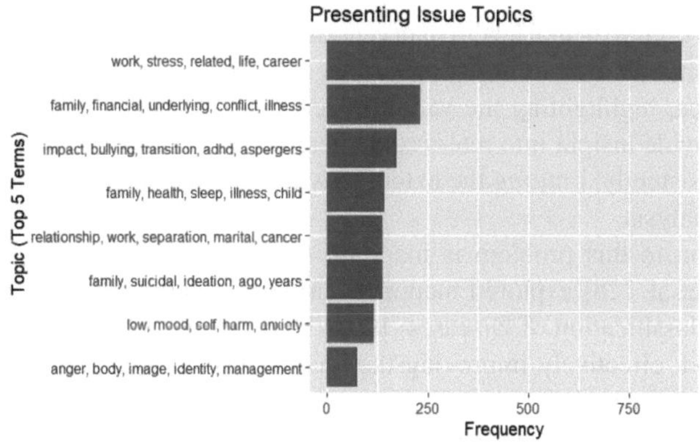

Fig. 3. Topic (and their top 5 terms) frequency in the dataset

4 Discussion

4.1 Use of Topic Modelling with EAP Counselling Presenting Issues

This study explored the application of topic modelling to a large corpus of client-reported mental health presenting issues, at the point of referral, with a focus on the small proportion of entries submitted in a free-text format by counsellors. Although this section of the dataset made up only 0.62% (n = 1126) of entries, analysis of them offered insights into presenting issues that may not be adequately captured in the predefined categories provided. Focusing on the narrative driven problem statements enabled a more meaningful analysis of topics within the dataset.

Coherence scoring and visual inspection suggested an 8-topic solution was the best choice balancing granularity and interpretability. The most common themes identified in the dataset were labelled as follows: 1. Work-related stress and life pressures, 2. Family conflict, 3. Neurodiversity and transitions, 4. Family health and sleep, 5. Relationship breakdown and illness, 6. Suicidal Ideation, 7. Low mood and self-harm and 8. Anger and body image. Some of the topics may fit into the predefined categories already available, such as "Work/Academic" relating to "Work-related stress and life pressures", and "Interpersonal/Relationship" for "Relationship breakdown and illness". Analysis of common words utilised as presenting reasons show "family" as a highly weighted word within the dataset.

The model highlighted topics such as neurodiversity, and presenting issues around family and children's illness, which offer a more nuanced description than with the predefined categories. In practice, detail like this could inform service delivery, matching a client with a counsellor experienced in neurodiversity for example. Future validation should include inter-annotator agreement studies with counsellors to assess topic interpretability, and benchmarking against embedding-based topic models.

4.2 Alignment with Structured Taxonomies

One of the challenges in mental health services, particularly in nonclinical settings like EAPs, is the lack of standardised diagnostic language. A recent umbrella review on the effectiveness of digital mental health interventions for the workplace found the use of 108 outcome assessments used to measure various aspects of mental health and wellbeing in the workplace, highlighting the variation across assessments [27]. Whilst free text options can provide insight into real-world client concerns, they can be ambiguous and recorded inconsistently, limiting the extent to which trends and patterns can be derived through data analysis.

One solution to this problem is mapping free-text variables to ICD codes, such as Turkington et al. [28] explored mapping reasons for calling a crisis helpline to the International Classification of Diseases–10 (ICD-10). Xue and Lu [29] utilised a deep learning method, effectively improving the quality of ICD automatic mapping within electronic medical records.

While some EAP concerns such as "work stress" do not directly correspond to formal diagnoses, ICD-11 includes relevant entries under "Factors influencing health status" (e.g., QD83.1: Problems associated with stressful work schedule). These mappings are not diagnostic but serve to align presenting issues with recognised clinical classifications to support structured documentation and potential integration with health systems. Furthermore, EAP services are not designed to diagnose mental health conditions, and counsellors may avoid diagnostic labelling, mapping presenting issues to clinical taxonomies such as ICD categories offers a bridge to clinical systems and population level reporting.

4.3 Opportunities and Limitations of using LLMs in Mental Health

These findings from this topic modelling study using LDA can inform the basis of a LLM support tool, where counsellors are offered suggested structured categories to select from, if the presenting issue is quite ambiguous. The support tool may also suggest relevant resources, or care pathways based on real-time input from client narratives. By leveraging the results from the LDA analysis, and alignment with taxonomies, such a tool could generate structured suggestions, highlight common co-occurring concerns, and prompt further clarification when needed.

When surveyed on their awareness, attitudes and practices relating to chatbots, 77% of healthcare professionals believed that chatbots were very or somewhat important in mental health care and may assist mental healthcare workers in their daily roles [30]. To explore this idea, a proposed conversational interface design is outlined in Sect. 4.4.

However, the implementation of LLM-based tools within employee assistance programmes must be approached with caution. Responsible AI practices are essential to ensure the safe, equitable, and transparent use of such systems. The use of LLMs concerns about bias, misinterpretation, and overgeneralisation, especially when applied to sensitive, culturally specific, or emotionally nuanced narratives. In the next two sections, we will outline a proposed prototype for an LLM-based counsellor support tool for categorising presenting issues, and the responsible AI considerations that would need to be mitigated.

4.4 Proposed LLM-Based Tool for Counsellor Support and Assistance

Based on the thematic insights derived from topic modelling of free-text problem statements, we propose a prototype counsellor support tool that leverages LLMs to support mental health professionals in counselling and mental health settings. While structured data categories are widely used, they often fail to capture the nuance and ambiguity present in real-world client concerns. The proposed tool aims to bridge this gap by interpreting free-text entries, suggesting clinically meaningful categories (mapped to structured taxonomies such as ICD-11), and prompting clarification where needed. The International Classification of Diseases (ICD), currently in its 11th revision (ICD-11), is often associated with the classification of mental and behavioural disorders, which are organised into 21 high-level categories (e.g., depressive disorders, psychotic disorders, anxiety disorders). However, the ICD-11 also includes chapters for a wide range of health-related factors that are not diagnoses, but rather "factors influencing health status or contact with health services" (e.g., work-related stress, social issues, life events).

The support tool was conceptualised in a chatbot-style interface to mirror conversational triage practices. Table 2 contains illustrative examples demonstrating how the tool could respond to counsellor-entered free-text summaries.

Table 2. Suggested use cases for LLM-based counsellor support tool

Use Case	Counsellor Input	Support Tool Output:
1. Simple suggestion for structured taxonomy mapping	Client is experiencing ongoing stress due to workload and unrealistic deadlines. They're reporting sleep issues and trouble concentrating. What is the suggested presenting issue?	Suggested Categories: • Stressful work schedule (ICD-11: QD83.1) • Insomnia (ICD-11: 7A01) Confidence: High Note: Sleep issues and cognitive impairment frequently co-occur with occupational stress.
2. Multiple presenting issues	Client is grieving the loss of a parent and has also mentioned feeling isolated at work.	Suggested Categories: Primary Issue: • Grief (ICD-11: QE62) Secondary Issue: • Workplace social isolation (Closest is Problem associated with interpersonal interactions ICD-11: QE50) Confidence: High Would you like to explore possible support plans related to bereavement and social reintegration?

(continued)

Table 2. (*continued*)

Use Case	Counsellor Input	Support Tool Output:
3. Ambiguous or vague entry	Client said they're just 'not coping anymore' and feel overwhelmed	Possible Categories (based on semantic similarity): • Adjustment disorder, unspecified (ICD-11: 6B43.Z) • Mixed anxiety and depressive symptoms (ICD-11: 6A73) Confidence: Medium This phrase is broad. Would you like to expand with additional symptoms or context?

The tool may be presented in the form of a conversational agent, where counsellors enter summaries and receive interactive suggestions. Confidence levels and justification (e.g., "based on similar cases") being provided within the response may help maintain transparency and trust.

The tool could move beyond categorisation by suggesting potential pathways forward (e.g., related resources or care plans). In a production setting, the content used to generate these suggestions would need to be sourced from structured, clinically approved knowledge bases, such as internal documents currently used in counselling.

The topic labels and themes identified through LDA can form the foundation of the LLM's structured knowledge base, enabling retrieval-augmented generation (RAG) and prompt engineering to suggest appropriate classifications and resources based on counsellor-entered free text. The development and governance of this content would require input from clinical subject matter experts, regular review cycles, and robust version control to ensure relevance and safety. The tool would therefore function as a decision support system, not a treatment provider, always leaving the final judgment and action with the qualified counsellor.

Future work will involve consultation and if deemed a feasible and useful proposal, co-design with counsellors, and testing with anonymised cases. Evaluation metrics for such a tool could include mapping accuracy to ICD-11 categories, precision/recall of suggested classifications, and sensitivity in flagging high-risk cases. The aim is to co-develop a digital triage assistant that enhances human judgment, rather than replacing it, in mental health support.

4.5 Responsible AI Considerations

As AI becomes more integrated into our daily lives, and specifically in health care, it is paramount that such tools are ethically and responsibly designed, developed and deployed. This is especially important in the context of mental health, where we have already seen LLMs applied to sensitive client session notes, or deployed to support individuals through conversational interfaces. The proposed prototype in this study, an LLM-based support tool for assisting counsellors must be developed in alignment with the principles of Re-sponsible AI, including transparency, accountability, fairness, and respect for human dignity [31].

One of the main considerations when designing AI systems is data privacy, as without appropriate safeguards when training AI systems on data, the privacy rights of users may be violated [32]. To address this, development of the prototype must adhere to strict data protection protocols, such as General Data Protection Regulation (GDPR) alongside transparent user consent procedures, particularly if the tool is deployed in real-world settings such as an EAP.

Another main issue is the potential for bias. LLMs, including those fine-tuned for healthcare, are trained on massive datasets that can encode racial, gender, cultural, or diagnostic biases [33]. In mental health, this can manifest in the form of skewed suggestions or underrepresentation of culturally specific expressions of distress. To mitigate bias, the model should be trained with diverse training data and evaluated through regular bias audits. Involving domain experts and users from underrepresented populations during design and evaluation phases is essential for equitable model development [34].

Explainability and transparency within AI systems is vitally important, in order to maintain trust with the user. This proposed system must make it clear how the suggestions are generated, which could be done through confidence scores when mapping presenting issues to clinical taxonomies. This can help mental health professionals retain control over interpretation and foster trust in the tool.

Finally, the system should be deployed within a human-in-the-loop model, where outputs are always reviewed by qualified mental health professionals. This approach ensures accountability and human oversight, key tenets of Responsible AI [31], or the suggestions can be treated as recommendations by the counsellor to use, modify or ignore. The proposed prototype could assist triage or care planning but should never be used for automated diagnosis or high-risk decision-making. Flagging ambiguous or high-risk entries (e.g., suicidal ideation) for human review is a necessary safety mechanism [35]. This could be operationalised by ensuring such entries are automatically flagged for review by a senior clinician. Scenario-based testing with simulated high-risk inputs could be used to validate these guardrails, making the ethical framework concrete to prioritise client safety and counsellor accountability.

The proposed idea is to generate topic-aligned suggestions and mappings to known clinical taxonomies to support clinical thinking, rather than replace it. WHO [35] outline clear ethical and governance considerations on the use of AI in health, including preserving and enhancing human autonomy. AI technologies should be developed to enhance human decision-making and empower medical professionals rather than replace them. By integrating these principles from data ethics to transparency and human-centred design, the prototype has the potential to not only support clinical practice, but to do so in a way that prioritises patient safety, counsellor trust, and social responsibility.

5 Conclusion

The aim of this study was to reduce the dimensionality of presenting problems using topic modelling and explore the potential for LLMs to support counsellors with classifying a presenting issue, in line with more structured clinical taxonomies. To our knowledge, this is the first study using EAP data to classify presenting issues using machine learning approaches such as LDA.

These findings support the feasibility of dimensionality reduction for presenting issues and point to the value of assistive AI in supporting early-stage triage and referral. However, the deployment of such tools requires a commitment to responsible AI principles, clinician oversight, and rigorous evaluation. With careful co-design, development and deployment, and attention to ethical and responsible AI principles, such support tools may enhance triage accuracy, and support data-informed service planning.

5.1 Limitations

The main limitation of this study is that the main presenting reasons for each referral is recorded by the counsellor, who has the option to select from a predefined list or enter their own. Thus, the presenting issue may be influenced by the counsellor's perception. There is a sample bias, as the service is set within an employee assistance programme context, with employed individuals able to utilise the service.

From a methodological perspective, we employed Latent Dirichlet Allocation (LDA) for topic discovery due to its transparency and compatibility with our current IT infrastructure. More advanced embedding-based methods (e.g., BERTopic, contextualised topic models) may perform better, but these approaches are not yet feasible in our environment. We plan to explore them in future work as infrastructure constraints are lifted. One topic of "work-related stress" dominated the results, representing 46.5% of the dataset, which may be imbalanced but could reflect real-world prevalence as this dataset has been obtained from a workplace counselling service.

While results are promising, the diverse range of client statements and predominance of pre-selected categories restricted the volume of rich, free-text data available for modelling. Further work is needed to evaluate the clinical interpretability of the topics, compare alternative modelling approaches, and test the feasibility and safety of the proposed LLM-based support tool.

Acknowledgements. This work has been supported by the Industrial Fellowship programme by the Royal Commission for the Exhibition of 1851 and Lena (by Inspire).

Disclosure of interest. GC is an Industrial Fellow supported by the Royal Commission for the Exhibition of 1851 affiliated with Ulster University, and an employee in Lena (by Inspire), a mental health social enterprise, along with DC. There are no other conflicts of interest.

References

1. Rosso, B.D., Dekas, K.H., Wrzesniewski, A.: On the meaning of work: a theoretical integration and review. Res. Org. Behav. **30**, 91–127 (2010)

2. World Health Organization: World Health Organization -Mental health at work (2022). https://www.who.int/news-room/fact-sheets/detail/mental-health-at-work
3. Health and Safety Executive: Working days lost in Great Britain (2024). https://www.hse.gov.uk/statistics/dayslost.htm
4. Stevenson, D., Farmer, P.: Thriving at work: The Stevenson / Farmer review of mental health and employers (2017)
5. Joyce, S., et al.: Workplace interventions for common mental disorders: a systematic meta-review. Psychol. Med. **46**(4), 683–697 (2016)
6. Dewa, C.S., Thompson, A.H., Jacobs, P.: The association of treatment of depressive episodes and work productivity. Can. J. Psychiatry **56**(12), 743750 (2011)
7. Nankervis, A., Compton, R.L., McCarthy, T.E.: Strategic human resource management. South Melbourne: Thomas Nelson (1996). http://trove.nla.gov.au/work/3903432
8. Csiernik, R., Chaulk, P., McQuaid, S.: A process evaluation of a Canadian public sector employee assistance program. J. Work. Behav. Health **27**(3), 160–180 (2012). https://doi.org/10.1080/15555240.2012.701169
9. Martin, P., et al.: Developing a case mix classification for child and adolescent mental health services: the influence of presenting problems, complexity factors and service providers on number of appointments. J. Mental Health (Abingdon, England) **29**(4), 431–438 (2020). https://doi.org/10.1080/09638237.2017.1370631
10. Joseph, B., Walker, A., Fuller-Tyszkiewicz, M.: Evaluating the effectiveness of employee assistance programmes: a systematic review. Eur. J. Work Organ. Psy. **27**(1), 1–15 (2018)
11. Sahu, B., Kedia, J., Ranjan, V., Mahaptra, B.P., Dehuri, S.: Mental health prediction in students using data mining techniques. Open Bioinform. J. **16**(1) (2023)
12. Cameron, G., Cameron, D., Mulvenna, M., Bond, RR., Ennis, E., O'Neill, S.: Employee engagement with a digital wellbeing platform: insights from association rule mining analysis. In: 32nd Irish Conference on Artificial Intelligence and Cognitive Science, Dublin, Ireland (2024)
13. Cameron, G., et al.: Real-world usage of a digital employee wellbeing platform: k-means clustering analysis. In: 2024 IEEE International Conference on E-health Networking, Application & Services (HealthCom), pp. 1–4. IEEE (2024)
14. Barak-Corren, Y., et al.: Validation of an electronic health record–based suicide risk prediction modeling approach across multiple health care systems. JAMA Netw. Open **3**(3), e201262–e201262 (2020)
15. Husain, W., Xin, L.K., Rashid, N.A., Jothi, N.: Predicting generalized anxiety disorder among women using random forest approach. In: 2016 3rd Int Conf Comput Inf Sci., pp. 37–42 (2016)
16. Laricheva, M., Liu, Y., Shi, E., Wu, A.: Scoping review on natural language processing applications in counselling and psychotherapy. Br. J. Psychol. (2024)
17. Carron-Arthur, B., Reynolds, J., Bennett, K., Bennett, A., Griffiths, K.M.: What's all the talk about? Topic modelling in a mental health Internet support group. BMC Psychiatry **16**(1), 367 (2016)
18. Sik, D., Németh, R., Katona, E.: Topic modelling online depression forums: beyond narratives of self-objectification and self-blaming. J. Ment. Health **32**(2), 386–395 (2023)
19. Iyortsuun, N.K., Kim, S.H., Jhon, M., Yang, H.J., Pant, S.: A review of machine learning and deep learning approaches on mental health diagnosis. In: Healthcare, vol. 11, no. 3, p. 285. MDPI (2023)
20. Gunal, A., Lin, B., Bouneffouf, D.: Conversational topic recommendation in counseling and psychotherapy with decision transformer and large language models. arXiv preprint arXiv:2405.05060 (2024)
21. Guo, Z., Lai, A., Thygesen, J.H., Farrington, J., Keen, T., Li, K.: Large language model for mental health: a systematic review. arXiv 2024. arXiv preprint arXiv:2403.15401

22. Huang, L., et al.: A survey on hallucination in large language models: principles, taxonomy, challenges, and open questions. ACM Trans. Inf. Syst. **43**(2), 1–55 (2025)
23. Ranaldi, L., Pucci, G.: When large language models contradict humans? Large language models' sycophantic behaviour. arXiv preprint arXiv:2311.09410 (2023)
24. Carro, M.V.: Flattering to deceive: the impact of sycophantic behavior on user trust in large language model (2024). arXiv preprint arXiv:2412.02802
25. Li, L., Kong, S., Zhao, H., Li, C., Teng, Y., Wang, Y.: Chain of Risks Evaluation (CORE): a framework for safer large language models in public mental health. Psychiatry Clin. Neurosci. **79** (2025). https://doi.org/10.1111/pcn.13781
26. Blair, S.J., Bi, Y., Mulvenna, M.D.: Aggregated topic models for increasing social media topic coherence. Appl. Intell. **50**, 138–156 (2020). https://doi.org/10.1007/s10489-01901438-z
27. Cameron, G., et al.: Effectiveness of digital mental health interventions in the workplace: umbrella review of systematic reviews. JMIR Mental Health **12**(1), e67785 (2025)
28. Turkington, R., et al.: Why do people call crisis helplines? Identifying taxonomies of presenting reasons and discovering associations between these reasons. Health Inform. J. **26**(4), 2597–2613 (2020)
29. Xue, J., Lu, P.: ICD code mapping model based on clinical text tree structure. Artif. Intell. Med., 103163 (2025)
30. Sweeney, C., et al.: Can chatbots help support a person's mental health? Perceptions and views from mental healthcare professionals and experts. ACM Trans. Comput. Healthc. **2**(3), 1–15 (2021)
31. Floridi, L., et al.: AI4People—An ethical framework for a good AI society: opportunities, risks, principles, and recommendations. Mind. Mach. **28**(4), 689–707 (2018)
32. Price, W.N., Cohen, I.G.: Privacy in the age of medical big data. Nat. Med. **25**(1), 37–43 (2019)
33. Singhal, K., et al.: Large language models encode clinical knowledge. Nature **620**(7972), 172–180 (2023)
34. Jobin, A., Ienca, M., Vayena, E.: The global landscape of AI ethics guidelines. Nat. Mach. Intell. **1**(9), 389–399 (2019)
35. World Health Organization: Ethics and governance of artificial intelligence for health: Guidance on large multi-modal models (2025). https://www.who.int/publications/i/item/978924 0084759

The Politics of Defining AI: Discourse, Legitimacy, and the Ethics Crisis

Jess Haynie-Lavelle(✉)

Malmö University, Malmö, Sweden
jess.haynie-lavelle@mau.se

Abstract. Artificial Intelligence (AI) is a contested and rapidly evolving domain shaped by discourse, power, and historical narratives. Using Foucauldian genealogy, Bacchi's poststructural policy analysis, and Habermasian legitimacy theory, the analysis reveals how framing practices obscure ethical complexities while participatory sensemaking offers a more inclusive path forward. AI is not a fixed entity but a dynamic concept constructed through competing narratives and regulatory framings. Linguistic choices and policy discourse influence public perception, governance priorities, and the distribution of risks and benefits. The EU's AI Act exemplifies how normative assumptions and legitimation struggles manifest in transnational regulation. Ethical design of AI systems requires more than technical solutions—it demands democratic engagement, contextual awareness, and amplification of marginalized voices. By embracing discourse as a productive and contested process, ethical sensemaking can guide the development of AI systems that are transparent, just, and responsive to societal needs.

Keywords: Discourse · Framing · Sensemaking · Legitimacy · Regulation

1 Reframing AI Ethics Through Discourse

Artificial Intelligence (AI) is a rapidly evolving and contested domain that influences nearly every aspect of modern life. This paper critically examines the discursive construction of AI, exploring how language, power, and historical narratives shape our understanding of its ethical implications. Drawing on Foucauldian genealogy, Bacchi's poststructural policy analysis, and Habermasian legitimacy theory, the paper argues for a shift from authoritative framing to participatory sensemaking in AI governance. The structure of the paper is as follows: it begins with a theoretical framework distinguishing framing from sensemaking, followed by a genealogical analysis of AI discourse. It then explores the social structures and biases embedded in AI systems, examines the EU's regulatory framing through Bacchi's lens, and discusses global governance tensions. The paper concludes by proposing ethical sensemaking as a pathway to inclusive and democratic AI design.

The challenge of developing AI is not merely a technical or legal one; it is fundamentally a question of meaning. What do we mean when we talk about "artificial intelligence"? Who gets to decide how data is codified, or which systems are prioritised?

K. Nasrollahi et al. (Eds.): REPAI-W 2025, LNCS 16390, pp. 101–118, 2026.
https://doi.org/10.1007/978-3-032-16886-3_7

How do these organisational processes influence public perception, policy priorities, and the allocation of resources? These queries go to the heart of how societies make sense of technological interferences are allowed to distribute risks and benefits and imagine possible futures.

The complexity of the AI discourse is further compounded by the rapid pace of technological change and the global scale of AI's impact. The broad implementation of AI systems has been characterized by its speed, its reach, and its capacity to disrupt established social, economic, and political arrangements. The proliferation of AI systems in everyday life—from media recommendation algorithms and facial recognition to text prediction and automated hiring—has raised urgent questions about privacy, accountability, and democratic norms. These questions are not easily answered within existing regulatory frameworks designed for a pre-digital era. At the same time, the promise of AI as a tool for social good—capable of solving intractable problems and expanding human potential—remains a powerful motivator for continued investment and innovation.

In this context, the social management of AI technologies is both vital and fraught. On the one hand, there is a need for global frameworks to ensure that AI systems are developed and deployed in ways that respect fundamental rights. On the other hand, the very act of legislating AI is complicated by the fluidity of the concept itself, the diversity of its applications, and the speed at which the technology evolves.

This paper argues that effective AI solution setting requires a more nuanced and participatory approach to sensemaking—one that recognizes the limitations of existing frames, foregrounds the social and political dimensions of technological change to actively engage a broad range of stakeholders in the process of defining problems and crafting solutions. Rather than treating AI as a fixed and knowable entity, we must approach it as a dynamic and contested field, shaped by ongoing struggles over meaning, power, and legitimacy.

To this end, the paper is structured as follows. First, it explores the theoretical foundations of discourse analysis, highlighting the distinction between framing and sensemaking and their relevance to the AI debate. Next, it examines the historical and linguistic construction of AI, drawing on Foucault to trace narratives that reveal the societal impacts of AI, with a particular focus on issues of bias and justice. It then develops the challenges of emergent AI regulation, using Bacchi's WPR approach to expose the legislative framings with the European context. Drawing from the framings of AI narratives, the paper adopts a Habermasian critique of legitimacy to present the power imbalances within the regulation of AI in a rapidly changing and globally interconnected environment. Finally, the paper offers a critical discussion of current approaches to AI governance, identifying sensemaking opportunities for more ethical forms of regulation.

Through this discussion the paper seeks to contribute to a more critical and reflective conversation about the development of ethical design of AI systems that proliferate within a global market—one that moves beyond hype and fear, and toward a more just, transparent, and participatory future. By interrogating the language surrounding ideas of what AI systems are understood to be, we can begin to understand the power dynamics that shape our understanding of AI. Building on the theoretical foundations, the next section delves into the historical and linguistic construction of AI.

2 Framing Versus Sensemaking in AI Discourse

From its origins in mid-20th-century computer science, AI has been variously understood as a military tool, a scientific aspiration, a commercial product, a market predictor, a philosophical puzzle, and a cultural metaphor. Each of these framings has brought with it different visions of the future, different models of agency and responsibility, and different stakes for governance and regulation. The discursive history of AI is thus not a straightforward story of technological progress, but a complex tapestry of competing narratives, interests, and values.

In the realm of discourse analysis, the literature of sensemaking has been introduced as an element of social action, distinct from framing practices. Framing consists of focusing the attention onto a particular version of meaning and therefore evoking a power struggle for definition control (Benford & Snow, 2000). It can be understood as a highly political process which makes culture and society a contested terrain. Sensemaking is a narrative prompted by the contestation of framing, in that it seeks to identify the patterns of meaning through the environmental cues to develop a coherent account of what is really happening in society (Vaara & Whittle, 2022). How, then, can AI technologies be framed, or even contested into sensemaking, when we are without a sustainable definition of the term?

The lack of an agreed-upon global definition of AI systems frustrates discussions around what they might become, and how they should be treated within society and legislative processes. However, there are ideas that surround the technologies which impact conceptual associations. The words we use to describe AI—whether as *intelligent, reasoning, decision-making, planning, creativity, understanding, knowing, autonomous, perceive, problem-solving, adapting, analysing, smart, efficient* or *learning*—carry with them a host of assumptions, expectations, and anxieties. Like the technology they describe, these linguistic choices are not neutral. They are imbued with the power of social sensemaking, shaping the conversation of whose interests are prioritized, and what kinds of solutions are supported. As Michel Foucault and other theorists of discourse have argued, language does not merely reflect reality; it actively shapes it. As these words shape our collective understanding of our interactions with these technologies, what authorities have the right to define these concepts?

The history of thought about AI is not a linear progression but a series of discontinuous, purposeless processes shaped by language and power. The concepts around AI systems are not static; they are inherited, contested, and redefined through discourse. The power of language lies in its ability to reveal and structure our experience of the world, rather than simply moving thought forward. This perspective encourages a critical assessment of the utility and implications of the terms we use, and to consider how they shape public understanding and policy. For example, in using terminology associated with human intelligence and processes – such as *planning* or *creativity* – the AI systems are placed in competition with our own capabilities.

The power of discourse is therefore not the putting forward of individuals' concepts, handed down through intellectual inheritance, but rather as a messy, purposive-less, discontinuous process. This places a tension within our own human desires to create a goal-oriented narrative, but Foucault distinguishes this impulse from the general mode of thinking which shapes our understanding and moves discourse forward. "…there is no simple correspondence between a general structure of thought and specific beliefs and actions." (Gutting, 2005). Thus, while Artificial Intelligence could mean many things to many people, it has been framed to mean specific things within different contexts. Within the cultural sci-fi genre AI is a digitalised human, which undermines humanity. Within the military complex it is automated aviation or surveillance capabilities. Within the market economy, AI has come to mean efficiency. Thus, while the topic and term are the same, different environments frame our interpretation of the technologies' characteristics. Each definition does not need to agree with the other, as our human languages are contextual, messy and ever evolving. Nevertheless, the construction of meaning of AI systems actively shapes our everyday understandings of the technologies and our experiences of them.

Foucault made explicit the relationship between knowledge and power, drawing from Nietzschean genealogy to show how it is also utilized to evoke authority. Perhaps this is the source of the original fear of AI: if something *artificial* can process and hold more *intelligence* than a human, then how could we not be infantilized by its scope? The un-knowableness of AI sits very uncomfortably within us, and we discursively attribute an almost superhuman-like knowledge (and power) to the technology (Goode, 2018). However, through critiquing the sensemaking process, we can make its power visible and therefore contestable. Having established a few of the discursive roots of AI, we now turn to its societal impacts, focusing on how design and data practices perpetuate bias and inequality.

3 Social Structures of AI Systems

A history of thought can be told about AI in which it was established to account for the unknown potential of its technological development. As the works of Foucault remind us, our history is a stage on which we enact (Gutting, 2005). The concepts we entertain, which shape our understanding, and expression, of the present history and daily experience are inherited by us all. Their power is rooted in how they help us to continuously redefine the world around us. In this way words reveal the structure of the world around us, rather than as stand-alone concepts that move thought forward. Thus, when AI is associated with the potential for a Singularity (Goode, 2018), the development of Agentic AI is supported. While the concept of an independent intelligence which surpasses human intelligence is still theoretical, it holds space in our collective imagination and therefore structures how we respond to the potential of such a future. The concept may be experienced as threatening or hopeful, but it is nevertheless experienced as possible. Regardless of the messy contestation of the meaning and impact enacted on our social and political stages, without the imagination to conceive of a singularity, there would be no space for its future potential.

Central to the sensemaking process of AI systems is the claim to neutrality. AI is frequently presented as a neutral tool, capable of eliminating human bias from decision-making. However, AI systems are susceptible to the perpetuation and even amplification of existing social inequalities, particularly when biases are embedded in data or design (Alon-Barkat & Busuioc, 2021; Hao, 2019; Tilmes, 2022). The challenge to sensemaking of AI is not only technical but ethical and political, where justice and safety within AI systems is uncertain. Interventions to correct inequalities and prevent discrimination, must be grounded in a clear understanding of the social and normative dimensions of AI and our collective understanding of the data from which these technologies are developed.

The societal impact of AI cannot be understood in isolation from the broader context of existing global capitalist world-ordering. Where digital technologies are developed in an environment of *surveillance capitalism* (Zuboff, 2015), they will support and perpetuate these agendas. As Zuboff argues, the normalization of data extraction and commodification of human behaviour has profound implications for privacy, democracy, and individual autonomy. The lack of effective regulation has allowed corporations to shape digital systems according to their interests, often at the expense of human rights (Molnar, 2019) and democratic participation (König & Wenzelburger, 2020).

The tendency to focus on the outcomes of the technology, for example the technological object's effect or capability, without sensemaking it within the social processes is dangerous. The extractive design process of these technologies is intentional and consequential (Zuboff, 2015), yet the process is framed as a necessary exchange for accuracy (Alexander & Kate, 2020). Our collective sensemaking of these systematic organisations is overwhelmed by the sheer size and scope of data management, which translates every interaction into categorizable information to be capitalized upon. Predictive systems, for example, are framed as *recommendations* to users. Yet within online platforms alone, such 'choice architectures' have been demonstrated to manipulate thought of the users, thus undermining any alternative sensemaking (Teo, 2024). Users have their freedom of thought systematically moderated through their interactions with AI systems, which is designed to keep users maintaining the process of datafication to support a multi-billion-dollar annual industry (Crawford, 2021).

While this lack of personal privacy and unpaid human labour of data creation may be normalized, resulting harms against everyday people lack accountability measures (Bircan & Korkmaz, 2021; Zuboff, 2022). Regulation of these systems are localized and weak in relation to the private corporate social influence (Crawford, 2021; Ram, 2025). In scenarios where governance has yet to make explicit the applicable regulation, the corporations within the digital field rely on contractual arrangements to support their goals. Without the need to follow legal obligations, people are treated as consumers and enter a contractual relationship determined by the platform - largely without meaningful knowledge of the legitimacy of these contracts (Jones et al., 2018), or the information leaks of sensitive data (Samarin et al., 2024). The day-to-day result is a cycle of infringement without reciprocity to the people who are affected. Within this capitalist design for AI there exists no need for the everyday person's trust, which is a vital aspect in the contractual obligation of democratic societies. Untethered by regulatory obligations to mitigate inequitable harms, ethically designed AI is fundamentally not supported.

There exist three main areas of debate within the current discourse around AI regulation (Sampath, 2021). The first is around privacy and surveillance, how the data is collected and what spaces can be considered private are in question. The second is the ethical and responsible AI applications, which are often applied for attention directing (or misdirecting) and information manipulation. Finally, the opacity and bias built into AI systems is also in question. Bias stems from problems of lack of diversity in data sets, where certain categories of people tend to be overrepresented in different data sets (Benjamin, 2019; Caliskan et al., 2017; Coeckelbergh, 2022) and research accountability, where unintended consequences present themselves (Bontridder & Poullet, 2021; Brandsen et al., 2024).

An appeal often made to regulatory decision-makers is the potential for AI to act as a tool without human bias. It is lauded as a vehicle by which consistent and fair calculations can be conducted, allowing for a confidence in super-human predictive processes. While in theory this fairytale ending could be dream come true, the current reality must account for the human developers and human generated data which inextricably insert ethical harms into AI systems. AI systems have begun to inhabit the basic structure of our global societies and regulation of their activity is not matched to the real and potential everyday experience of their harms. To understand how discourse translates into policy, the following section analyses the EU's AI Act, revealing the normative assumptions embedded in regulatory language.

4 EU Regulatory Narratives

The EU, like many other authorities, has declared the daily importance of AI technologies on our everyday lives; "The way we approach Artificial Intelligence (AI) will define the world we live in the future" (European Commission, 2025a). The European Commission therefore was formed to undertake the development of the first regulations of AI systems. Through this process the agency adopted an authoritative role in the definition of AI, and therefore the future global politics. By looking into the terms used to describe AI systems, this section offers an epistemic value to problematize what the EU Parliament seeks to undergo. As the EU lays the groundwork for the regulation of AI, we would benefit from investigating how and why their particular framing of AI is proffered.

The EU's AI Act was born out of a response to the need for safeguarding against harms. The evidence of the bias built into AI systems is mounting and human reliance on the technology calls into question our democratic processes by entrenching inequalities into all our social systems (Gabriel, 2022). The European Commission frames the discussion of AI regulation in terms of trust: "The aim of the rules is to foster trustworthy AI in Europe."(European Commission, 2024a). The *Ethics guidelines for trustworthy AI* frames the process as an impact-assessment of Human agency, Robustness and safety, Privacy and data governance, Transparency, Diversity, Non-discrimination and fairness, Societal and environmental well-being, and Accountability (European Commission, 2019). The EU's AI Liability Directive (European Commission, 2022) was adopted to address trust – in the form of liability – of European corporate adoption of AI technologies; "the Commission undertook to promote the uptake of AI and to address the risks associated with some of its uses by fostering excellence and trust" (ibid, p.1).

A word frequency analysis of the reports referenced above (European Commission, 2022, 2024a; European Commission, 2019) reveals the regulation of AI continues to be framed in terms of trust. The emphasis on the *rights* of *humanity*, the *requirements* and *liability* concerns for a *trustworthy* technology arrive within the first five most frequently mentioned words[1]. The EU Commission's call to guidelines for *trustworthy* AI points to its opposite - an underlying fear of *untrustworthy* AI. The framing that AI has the potential to be trustworthy, and is therefore potentially untrustworthy, made the risk-based assessment model of the EU AI Act possible. Without the presence of this fear, or threat of AI systems, the regulatory management of risk would not be legitimised; "certain AI systems create risks that we must address to avoid undesirable outcomes" (European Commission, 2024a). The EU's adoption of risk-based categorization of AI systems, and their call to trustworthy technology problematizes AI technologies.

The framework of analysis offered by Carol Bacchi in her Poststructural Policy Analysis (2016) is laid out succinctly in seven not-so-simple steps. The first question has become iconic since its inception (Bacchi, 2009): What is the problem represented to be? Here she asks what is *the problem* that the policy seeks to address. To expand on the application of this analytical methodology, let us employ the example of AI regulation, to which I will rely on Explanatory Memorandum of the AI Act (European Commission, 2022). Here the problem is represented as the missing "legislation for a coordinated European approach on the human and ethical implications of AI" (ibid, p.1). This tells us that the EU Parliament: 1. Sees the legislative approach to AI systems as disjointed, 2. Claims an authority to coordinate a solution, 3. Mistrusts the human implications of AI, 4. Mistrusts the ethical implications of AI, and 5. AI is perceived as the source of the problem.

Bacchi's methodology is intended to function as a lever to open reflections about what is known, and how is it knowable. It asks us to work backwards from the solutions (policy development) to the problematization. The usefulness of the process is not merely to be a critical function, but also to query if alternatives may present themselves. By reflecting on what 'has to be' we may consider what alternatives may develop. Discourse is therefore understood as inherently productive, in that through language knowledge-production and reality-formation take place. Bacchi depicts discourse as the background knowledge that we participate within and therefore is it neither stagnant nor permanent, it also lacks a prime mover, as it is the ongoing process. Discourse is seen as a social production

---

[1] Word frequency analysis performed via Nvivo, applied to the following three references. European Commission. (2022). EXPLANATORY MEMORANDUM: DIRECTIVE OF THE EUROPEAN PARLIAMENT AND OF THE COUNCIL on adapting non-contractual civil liability rules to artificial ntelligence (AI Liability Directive). Brussels, European Commission. (2024a). Shaping Europe's digital future: AI Act. https://digital-strategy.ec.europa.eu/en/policies/regulatory-framework-ai, European Commission, H.-L. E. G. o. A. (2019). Ethics guidelines for trustworthy AI.These three references were selected for their visibility and relevance within the European Commission for AI ethics and liability regulations and public communications. The query included stemmed words and removed words shorter than four characters long and automatic stop words, such as "the". Nvivo generated summary is provided below.

Summary Word Cloud

Word	Length	Count	Weighted Percentage	Similar Words
rights	6	175	0,81%	right, rights, rights', rights'
humans'	7	164	0,76%	human, humanity, humans, humans'
liability	9	149	0,69%	liability, liability'
requires	8	145	0,67%	require, required, requirement, requirements,...
trustworthy	11	144	0,67%	trustworthiness, trustworthy

which delineates what is knowable and sayable. It is therefore a powerful practice of representing and producing the "real". Thus through the establishment of discursive fear of the un*trust*worthiness of AI technologies, the Parliament presents the problem of AI technologies as *requiring* their intervention in order to uphold the *liability* issues and ethical implications of *human rights*.

The concept of an ethical AI design is compelling to the normative values of European states, as part of their bid towards a democratically governed world, with European values centered within this political organisation. The legitimation of the legislation is rooted in two primary (unquestioned) concerns 1. The "establishment and functioning of the internal market" (ibid, p. 6) and 2. "the fundamental rights obligations" (ibid.) of the EU Charter. The normalization of EU values and goals towards the legislation of AI technologies is therefore based in unquestioned authority of the EU to enforce regulation on its member states (with implications on all those who move and trade within the EU).

When the EU agreed upon the Digital Services Act (DSA) (European Parliament, 2022) it was intended as a legislative framework that hoped to shape the global standard for safe digital spaces (El-Darwiche & Macpherson, 2021). The DSA has been in negotiations for years and a few smaller commissions were passed through the parliament, problematizing the roles of digital tools and services, such as the GDPR (European Parliament, 2016) and subsequently the creation of the High-Level Expert Group on AI (European Commission, 2019) for the development of the EU AI Act. Within the latter, the commission proposed a law for Europe to be the first major piece of AI regulation, with the goal of making it the global gold standard. The power enacted in this legislative move was to position the EU as single market of regulated AI technologies. Thus, the EU positioned itself as a authoritative regional power, while simultaneously crowding out potential influence from alternative power structures, such as foreign markets or governmental authorities.

Bacchi relates the role of policy in the practice of authority, where policy is understood to be a program of conduct used to wield existent power (Bacchi & Goodwin, 2016). Within the discursive development of these legislative acts there is the accounting for (and familiarity with) the historical and contemporary narratives that have outlined the relationships between nation states. The homepage explicitly states the Commission's role in upholding democratic policies; "Protecting our democracy, upholding our values" (European Commission, 2025b). According to Bacchi, legislation, which is born out of power conflict, cannot be accepted in absentia of the contextual relationships which look backwards through the discursive paths to conceive of and establish acceptable policy. The conflict of trust – and the lack thereof – of foreign markets and foreign governments having been established, the EU AI Act could be established to adopt a formative hand in the regulation of AI technologies.

The EU AI Act was developed from the discourse of trustworthiness of AI through an alignment with European democratic values. Adopting Bacchi's WPR approach in a word frequency analysis of the AI Act[2], the question is: If the EU AI Act is the first global regulation of AI technologies, what framing is offered to represent the problem?

[2] Word frequency analysis performed via Nvivo, applied to the following reference. Regulation (EU) 2024/1689, EU Artificial Intelligence Act, 144 (2024). https://artificialintelligenceact.eu/ai-act-explorer/The query included stemmed words and removed words shorter than four

The analysis did not return the word *trust*, but rather emphasised it's counterpart: risk. The term *risk* is indicative of the threat to the European democratic values previously established within the discourse of AI technologies. Following the analysis, the AI Act seeks to create some management of the AI systems which could be a *risk* to the *authorities*, *persons*, *data*, and *markets* within the European Union. This argument is in line with the constructed discourse the EU Parliament has been developing through the publications, press releases, communications, and reports prior to the legislation (European Commission, 2025a).

The EU AI Act is a definitive piece of discourse that establishes the sayability of EU Parliament as a legitimate authority in the interpretation of what AI technologies are, and, through legislative framing, how they should be understood. If the Union is accepted as legitimate, then it is acceptable to frame AI in the normative values and terms set by this authority.

The desire of the EU to be a global leader in the regulation of AI is not an accident, it is an intentional positioning of power to shape the conversation for its own inner stability. The interconnection between power and knowledge are what is most enlightening to this discussion of the legitimacy of the term Artificial Intelligence. The many calls for its definition have been filled and yet we are unsatisfied with the response. With the EU as an example, the definition of AI is providing an epistemic role, so that through classification it also seeks to produce knowledge about what AI can be. There are two salient points to address here, first is what is understood as AI, and the second is who - or what - the AI Act attempts to regulate. Ultimately the regulation applies to *persons*, *data* and *markets*, but, in a transnational digital arena, such enforcement is practically impossible. Therefore, the policy problematizes the creations, rather than the culprits.

AI technologies are represented as the problem, in as they embody the risks to European democratic values. Through this framing the liability of persons, data, and markets are secondary. This is akin to censoring the hate speech without redress to the writer. The EU AI Act problematises the wrong culprit, as the AI technologies are creations from environments of social inequalities and embedded biases. While free speech is a democratic tenant, hate speech laws have demonstrated that even democratic

---

characters long and automatic stop words, such as "the". Nvivo generated summary is provided below.

Summary | Word Cloud

Word	Length	Count	Weighted Percentage	Similar Words
risk'	5	763	1,75%	risk, risks, risk'
authorities	11	523	1,20%	authorities, authorities', authority, authority',...
persons	7	460	1,05%	person, personal, personality, persons, perso...
data'	5	418	0,96%	data, data'
market'	7	404	0,93%	market, marketing, markets, market'

After reviewing the associated references to each of the top 50 words, the following were removed: Union; council; parliament; European; Commission; member (related to the EU Parliament regulatory bodies); High (related to high-risk); System, model (related AI systems);Regulation (related to this piece of legislation); Body, general, purpose, service (non-signifier); Annex; article; point (used as referencing definitions). Removed verbs, as looking for signifiers of meaning, not action: Take; Placed; Deploy; Ensure; Notify; Using; Refer; Including; Provide; Application. Despite these adjustments the word "trust", or its similar words, were not represented within the word frequency analysis.

societies have limits to their tolerance. 'When is enough (risk) enough?' is what this legislation is implicitly asking. Simultaneously the EU is positioning itself to establish the boundaries of their authority to define the risks.

The global regulation of AI is fragmented at best and fails to organize itself into a cohesive structure. The EU parliament is attempting to formulate the global gold standard, but struggles to find cohesion among the diversity of social, economic and political process within Europe alone. The additional challenge of global recognition of heterogenous legislation is faced by the opposition of national goals and values, present in the discourse of transnational diplomacy. The EU's AI Act has been lauded as a line in the sand against untrustworthy AI, but, without global legitimation, a wave of resistance can easily wash it away. Expanding the regulatory lens, we explore the legitimacy challenges faced by governments in the digital age, drawing on Habermas to suppliment Foucauldian and Bacchian critiques.

5 Legitimacy Crisis Within Discourse

Foucauldian and Bacchian frameworks offer a poststructural critique of discourse and power that contrasts sharply with Habermas's normative theory of communicative action and legitimacy. Foucault's genealogical method views discourse as a discontinuous, purposeless process shaped by power relations rather than rational consensus. Power, in this view, is not centralized or inherently negative but relational and productive—it constitutes knowledge and social reality through language. Bacchi builds on this by emphasizing how policy discourse constructs problems rather than merely responding to them. Her "What's the problem represented to be?" (Bacchi, 2009) approach reveals how governance operates through framing, often silencing alternative interpretations and reinforcing dominant ideologies. In contrast, Jürgen Habermas theorizes discourse as a vehicle for rational deliberation within the public sphere (Habermas, 1975). His concern is that there is legitimation crisis in advanced capitalism, where political and economic systems merge, which threatens democratic participation. Habermas sees communicative rationality as a means to restore legitimacy through consensus and procedural justice. While Foucault and Bacchi question the very foundations of what is considered "sayable" or "knowable," Habermas seeks to preserve the possibility of a shared construction of understanding and normative agreement. It would be a mistake to underestimate the power of the systematisation of normative values (Zürn, 2018) that is enacted in governmental discourse. In the context of AI governance, Foucauldian and Bacchian approaches expose the framing mechanisms behind and within regulation, while Habermas offers a framework for understanding the processes of governmental legitimacy.

Habermas' depiction of governmental power comes from its ability to avoid instability, and as such its ability to navigate legitimation crisis. Within the framing of AI technologies - which yet remains largely undefined, unregulated and undetermined - the role of stability is a precarious endeavour. The advanced capitalist system outlined by Habermas was analysed from the viewpoints of the systems of economy, administration, legitimation, and class structure. Within the advanced capitalist system the division between the public and private economic system recoupled, so that the government - previously understood to be an intervening authority between citizen and market - now actively partakes to shape and stabilize of national economy. This dynamic has created legitimation problems, as the political and economic goals have merged, conflating their agendas.

The problem of legitimation is relevant to global political stability. It is the process by which governments appeal and cajole their populace with uncontested rule. Without a functioning legitimation process, a crisis will ensue. This crisis can take many forms, but if unresolved can lead to an overturn of the governmental structure and in some cases result in violence (Habermas, 1975). While it is an old tale, the current lack of legitimation can perhaps be a useful lens to understand the current global political polarization (Marino et al., 2024) crises experienced today. To take on the digital age, various governmental and non governmental powers are positioning themselves as the legitimate holders of authority on the definition of what AI is and could become. This reveals an interesting global tension as the technology, which was previously unregulated, is being differently delimited by these defining practices.

As new legislation takes shape to further insert governmental powers where there were none, a legitimation crisis over governmental interference in the economic and social arenas has ensued. We are witnessing this play out currently as governments struggle to define AI and their role in managing the digital spaces which have grown to have individual importance on the quality of our daily lives. The role of norms becomes most apparent when new legislation is being developed, as the built-in values and goals are made visible through problematization and discourse. To put the EU's framing of AI legislation in contrast with another global power, the American government, as of the end of 2025, as been redicent to offer regulation of any kind. While European discourse was shaped around ideas of risks or threats to democratic values, the "American AI Action Plan" emphasises the need to act[3]. Instead of a fear-based framing of limiting technologies, it adopts an industrious narrative of construction. Both authorities are concerned with the management of data, but the framing of AI legislation is very disparate otherwise. The White House has actively chosen not to formulate legislation, instead relying

[3] Word frequency analysis performed via Nvivo, applied to the following reference. Executive Office of the President of the United States (2025). *Winning the Race. America's AI Action Plan.* The White House Retrieved from www.whitehouse.govThe query included stemmed words and removed words shorter than four characters long and automatic stop words, such as "the". Nvivo generated summary is provided below. After reviewing the associated references to each of the top 50 words, the following were removed: federal, national, government, America, American, agencies, states, united, office, executive, NIST (the National Institute of Standards and Technology) (related to the USA regulatory bodies); policy, plan (in reference to the same text), program (noun used with different meanings, non-signifier), 2025. Despite the adjustments the word "risk" was not within the first 30 words, and the word "trust" appears only three times time throughout the text.

Summary Word Cloud

Word	Length	Count	Weighted Percentage	Similar Words
action	6	78	1,33%	action, actionable, actions
security	8	60	1,02%	secure, securities, security
development	11	57	0,97%	develop, developed, developer, developers,...
technology	10	52	0,88%	technological, technologies, technology
data	4	39	0,66%	data

on policy to influence the emergent industry towards the development of a competitive American market. This act alone communicates an acceptance of unregulated growth of the AI market, but the language within the policy mirrors a push towards building innovating technologies within the American context (Executive Office of the President of the United States, 2025). Where the EU Parliament seeks to build its legitimation on the basis of European democratic values to mitigate the risks of the market, the White House within Trump's presidency constructs its legitimacy on the grounds of public-private partnerships. According to a Habermasian read of this scenario, the stability of the American national economy makes the Trump presidency somewhat more vulnerable to a crisis of legitimation than the EU counterparts which connect their discourse to a code of trustworthy conduct.

Habermas laid out the problems to growth in the advanced capitalist system, including ecological, anthropological, and international balance in 1975. The balance of international powers is particularly salient in the political management of AI technologies, as transnational companies, interests, and technologies question the legitimacy of traditionally geo-politically rooted legislation. Within the discursive development of the definition and meaning of Artificial Intelligence, the private market is central. Global regulatory governance of the private market interest is lacking. The result is as Habermas warns – government legitimacy is tied to the economic performance of the region, and simultaniously undermined by a weakened political economy to manage the circulation of AI products within their market.

As governments seek to frame AI and digital technologies, they face a legitimation crisis: how to assert authority in the face of rapid technological change and transnational corporate power. Regulatory efforts are often fragmented and struggle to keep pace with technological and societal change. Democracy is often invoked as a solution, but participation is frequently passive, with real power concentrated among those with resource ownership. The digital age intensifies these challenges, as traditional governance structures struggle to keep pace with global, networked, datafied technologies. Definitions of AI serve not only technical but political and epistemic functions, shaping what is knowable and actionable. Currently the discourse around AI is being shaped by power relations, epistemic authority, and the struggle for legitimation.

6 Discourse as Governance

The regulation of digital spaces is fragmented and reactive, with corporations often acting as de facto regulators. The tension between free speech and the need to prevent harm is a persistent challenge, complicated by the global reach of digital platforms and the diversity of regulatory contexts. The lack of a cohesive global framework for digital governance leaves individuals vulnerable to rights infringements and undermines democratic processes. The problem of accountability is especially acute, as transnational digital processes blur the boundaries of responsibility and jurisdiction.

As discourse is understood to be productive of emergent normative themes and ideas, we turn to David Kaye (Kaye, 2019) to offer insight on the global struggle to enact digital governance. The actors at play in Kaye's text are the global instances of regulation around the language within the internet and the increasing call to digital regulation by EU members witnessed in the years leading up to the publication of his book. He problematizes the interplay of speech with the regulation of democratic values most explicitly. The actors are set on a global stage, so they query similar topics from multiple regulatory contexts. The regulatory body, or lack thereof, responsible for digital regulation varies somewhat from the AI regulation debate, but the tensions at play remain the same.

The problem is twofold according to Kaye. The first problem is the use of censorship as a tool or as repression. This dynamic is endogenous with democracy and the topic of "free speech" is epistemically connected to a democratically functioning society. The second problem is that of fragmentation of regulatory bodies, and the inability to form a kind of globalized regulation. The EU AI Act makes explicit the need to combat fragmentation and increase legal certainty (European Parliament, 2024). America's AI Action Plan, by contrast, frames the AI market as an arena for competition where the USA is expected to maintain dominance (Executive Office of the President of the United States, 2025). The dynamic of human values and goals, a highly contextual endeavour, is made explicit in Kaye's book through purposeful examples that are more than anecdotal, they offer insight to turning points of regulation.

Kaye is clear that, within certain contexts, the corporate interests are placed in the role of governance as arbitrators of discourse. Thus private actors are not governing their citizens, yet they are able to impose controls on their users; all the while claiming the role of platform as a non-editorial body. This is where the EU Parliament perceived a mounting need to intervene into the market and enact regulation to "ensure that AI systems placed on the Union market and used are safe and respect existing law on fundamental rights and Union values"(European Parliament, 2021). While there exists a sustained political will to assess the risk posed by AI systems, and have a legal response and regulatory framework in which to sieve the trustworthiness and risk to Union values, the problem is that the legitimacy of EU Parliament is, albeit to a lesser degree than the American government, inextricably linked to the stability of the European market.

The problem of accountability and responsibility are especially confounded due to the lack of geopolitical placements that transnational digital processes facilitate (Zuboff, 2015). There are few cases where platforms can be held to account (in very limited terms). Immediate accountability of corporations is to its shareholders, where as a government's accountability is to its citizens. Offending material generates revenue-creating engagement, so that corporations are financially incentivized to prioritize offending material (Kaye, 2019). The political economy of corporate interests to exercise power is underlined on the global stage. Both for the ability to govern users within the platforms and for ideological shaping to be better consumers. What is distinct from nation-state governance to digital governance is not only the latter's global application, but also its transnational actors: individual, governmental and corporate.

Kaye is not diving into the deep systematic processes of global governance but rather pointing to the discourse around the issues. Through the examples and experience as working as adjunct to the EU, the book shows how the political process of regulating speech on the internet was undermined by corporate interests. When powerful individuals are responsible for the management of the major information highways, how can global governance ethically manage the parameters of free speech? Kaye seems to be saying that with new technologies we continue to have the same human governance problems, but with the difficulty of locating who are the responsible and accountable agents. The old methods of corporate responsibility are failing citizen health and impacting democratic processes, what then is the responsibility of governance to intervene? How can global approaches be formed in the wake of varied agendas and when will the power of management be wrested from the corporations that profit the most from them?

This paper has thus far explored the tensions present in the framing of AI technologies. The discourses surrounding AI development, implementation, and regulation are the foundations for shaping our global societies. From linguistic analysis to regulatory and governance challenges, the paper claims that these discourses reveal the potential vulnerabilities of governmental legitimacy. The following section will return to the operationalisation of sensemaking as a tool for the creation of meaningful deliberation. While corporate and public authoritative framing offers terms in which to understand AI technologies, they have failed to offer an environment that is not continuously enacting harms on global populations. Sensemaking offers a shift through which AI technologies might be developed to serve the public good and reflect diverse human values.

7 Towards Ethical Sensemaking

Ethical sensemaking in practice requires more than technical fixes or top-down regulation—it demands inclusive deliberation that foregrounds human values, contextual understanding, and democratic participation. This means engaging diverse stakeholders in defining problems, designing solutions, and evaluating outcomes. It involves creating spaces for dialogue where competing narratives can be negotiated and where marginalized voices are amplified and empowered. By embracing discourse as a dynamic and contested process, ethical sensemaking can guide the development of AI systems that are, not only effective, but also just, transparent, and responsive to societal needs.

How can AI be ethically designed if we can't even discuss it? The discourse around AI has been forming into a fear of the too-intelligent for humans to comprehend. However, the lack of transparency accounts for the unknowability of these systems (Bontridder & Poullet, 2021). The EU Digital Services Act addresses precisely this insecurity, where the lack of data traceability is at odds with the trustworthiness of the systems. The problem is not that the system itself is not transparent - it is rather that we humans are not transparent to even ourselves. Human cultures have yet to form a society where the *rules of the game* are equitable (McCrory, 2024). While our societies remain inequitable, unethical outcomes will present themselves in AI systems (Ram, 2025). As inequalities are baked into our social systems, and data is created from these environments, the language of bias is inextricable from the design and development of AI systems. The "black box" problem—the opacity of AI systems—limits public understanding and oversight. Therefore, what should be discussed and problematized is the invisible hand of human codification and classification that engineers inequality (Benjamin, 2019) into our digital systems.

At the core of this inquiry was the distinction between framing and sensemaking—two concepts drawn from discourse analysis that help illuminate the dynamics at play in the AI narratives. Framing refers to the process by which certain aspects of reality are highlighted while others are obscured, according to specific interests or agendas. In the context of AI, framing can be seen in the way media, policymakers, and industry leaders emphasize certain narratives—such as the presence of disinformation (Bontridder & Poullet, 2021) or the promise of healthcare efficiency (Vikhrov et al., 2021)—while downplaying others, such as the mundane realities of algorithmic bias (Hintz et al., 2018) or the extractive practices of data collection (Crawford, 2021). Framing is thus a political act, one that shapes not only what is discussed, but also how it is discussed and who is included in the conversation.

Sensemaking, by contrast, is a more collective process. It involves the ongoing negotiation of meaning among diverse actors, each contributing their own experiences, values, and perspectives. Sensemaking is less about imposing a singular narrative and more about constructing a shared understanding that can accommodate complexity, disagreement and negotiation. In our globalized present and future, we require the ability to navigate varied norms and contexts to manage social interactions and mediations of AI systems. In the case of AI, sensemaking requires us to move beyond simplistic framing and engage with the messy, contested, and evolving nature of technological social change.

Making sense of AI technologies requires a dundamentally non-traditional approach to definition forming along power structures. The Foucaultian reading of the relationship between knowledge and power, where definition setting is akin to the embodiment of authority, has explained why global governances strive to control the AI narratives. However, the technologies are a part of our everyday experience; giving each of us the epistemic authority to co-define the meaning and future of AI technologies. However, the everyday voice is lacking within these legislative debates. The challenge is not that diverse, everyday, active participation in the term-setting of AI technologies does not exist. The challenge is that these perspectives are not being integrated into the conversations of AI regulation in meaningful terms.

The EU Parliament has made a claim to engage stakeholders through its voluntary initiative "AI Pact" (European Commission, 2024a) in which their experiences with the legislation will be gathered and shared. Without entering into a critical analysis of the elements of diversity of the stakeholders, what organisations and industries they are representing, how they are invited into these spaces, how stakeholder input is balanced with corporate interests, or why the exchange is based within a webinar platform (European Commission, 2024b) – stakeholders are still expected to operate within the established discourse of the European Commission's framing of AI technologies.

While legislative discussions continue to be centered around a risk-based analysis, opportunities for alternative discourses are crowded out. A rights-based regulation strategy, for example, could bring to light the everyday need to adopt participatory governance programmes within the design process to ensure data protection (McCrory, 2024). A sustainability-based regulation strategy could lift up the management of factors impacting our global environment (Cowls et al., 2021). A information-based approach could mitigate the increasing cognitive deficit of citizens and decision-makers within our political systems (König & Wenzelburger, 2020). A morality-based approach could highlight the cultural points of conflict which work against a unified framework in the management of AI systems (Ram, 2025). A development-based approach could support alternative conceptualisations of industrialisation (Sampath, 2021). A health-based approach could validate the continuous contestation of values "between public and private, state and market" (Strange, 2024). None of these productive approaches can be adopted while risk-based analysis continues to be the focus within the European Commission.

A sensemaking strategy calls for the uncomfortable, messy, and time consuming process of restructing decision-making authorities to include social action. The framing of AI technologies, and their regulatory management systems, would benefit from sensemaking contestations. As the EU AI Act continue is process of implementation, it remains to been seen what impact assessments of the legislations will be produced. Nevertheless, the epistemic value of discourse setting has revealed that the framing adopted within this piece of legislation will inherently have social impacts. Without undertaking a process of sensemaking, it seems unlikely that AI-produced harms can be entirely managed within the European context, let alone the global context. What AI technologies are, and what they could be, are questions that remain unanswered, but hopefully this paper has contributed to the validity of having critical discussions about their framing.

Disclosure of Interests. The author has no competing interests to declare that are relevant to the content of this article.

References

Alexander, C., Kate, C.: Enchanted determinism: power without responsibility in artificial intelligence. In: Engaging Science, Technology, and Society, vol. 6, pp. 1–19. Society for Social Studies of Science (2020)

Alon-Barkat, S., Busuioc, M.: Human-AI Interactions in Public Sector Decision-Making: 'Automation Bias' and 'Selective Adherence' to Algorithmic Advice (2021)

Bacchi, C., Goodwin, S.: Poststructural Policy Analysis: A Guide to Practice, 1st edn. Palgrave Macmillan (2016). https://research.ebsco.com/linkprocessor/plink?id=61ec9a98-e3b4-32f7-a662-6a05fe7a7528

Bacchi, C.L.: Analysing Policy: What's the Problem Represented to Be? / Carol Bacchi. Pearson (2009). https://research.ebsco.com/linkprocessor/plink?id=cfc72602-f39f-31c6-a511-30b9674c82a2

Benford, R.D., Snow, D.A.: Framing processes and social movements: an overview and assessment. Ann. Rev. Sociol. **26**, 611–639 (2000)

Benjamin, R.: Race after technology: Abolitionist Tools for the New Jim Code. Polity (2019). https://scholar.google.com/citations?view_op=view_citation&hl=en&user=XlsH9jEAAAAJ&citation_for_view=XlsH9jEAAAAJ:ULOm3_A8WrAC

Bircan, T., Korkmaz, E.E.: Big data for whose sake? Governing migration through artificial intelligence. Humanit. Soc. Sci. Commun. **8**(1), 241 (2021). https://doi.org/10.1057/s41599-021-00910-x

Bontridder, N., Poullet, Y.: The role of artificial intelligence in disinformation. Data Policy **3**, e32 (2021). https://doi.org/10.1017/dap.2021.20. Article e32

Brandsen, S., Chandrasekhar, T., Franz, L., Grapel, J., Dawson, G., Carlson, D.: Prevalence of bias against neurodivergence-related terms in artificial intelligence language models. Autism Res. Off. J. Int. Soc. Autism Res. **17**(2), 234–248 (2024). https://doi.org/10.1002/aur.3094

Caliskan, A., Bryson, J.J., Narayanan, A.: Semantics derived automatically from language corpora contain human-like biases. Science **356**(6334), 183–186 (2017)

Coeckelbergh, M.: The Political Philosophy of AI: An Introduction. Polity Press (2022)

Cowls, J., Tsamados, A., Taddeo, M., Floridi, L.: The AI gambit: leveraging artificial intelligence to combat climate change-opportunities, challenges, and recommendations. AI Soc., 1–25 (2021). https://doi.org/10.1007/s00146-021-01294-x

Crawford, K.: The Atlas of AI: Power, Politics, and the Planetary Costs of Artificial Intelligence, 1st edn. Yale University Press (2021)

El-Darwiche, B., Macpherson, A.: The Digital Services Acts Package and what it entails. *PwC.com* (2021). https://www.pwc.com/m1/en/publications/documents/the-digital-services-acts-package.pdf. Accessed 25 Apr 2022

European Commission: EXPLANATORY MEMORANDUM: DIRECTIVE OF THE EUROPEAN PARLIAMENT AND OF THE COUNCIL on adapting non-contractual civil liability rules to artificial ntelligence (AI Liability Directive). Brussels (2022)

European Commission: Shaping Europe's digital future: AI Act (2024a). https://digital-strategy.ec.europa.eu/en/policies/regulatory-framework-ai

European Commission: Shaping Europe's digital future: AI Pact (2024b). https://digital-strategy.ec.europa.eu/en/policies/ai-pact

European Commission: European approach to artificial intelligence (2025a). https://digital-strategy.ec.europa.eu/en/policies/european-approach-artificial-intelligence

European Commission: European Commission homepage (2025b). https://commission.europa.eu/index_en

European Commission, H.-L. E. G. o. A.: Ethics guidelines for trustworthy AI (2019)

European Parliament, C. o. t. E. U.: Regulation (EU) 2016/679 of the European Parliament and to the Council on the protection of natural persons with regard to the processing of personal data (GDPR: General Data Protection Regulation) (2016). https://eur-lex.europa.eu/legal-content/EN/TXT/PDF/?uri=CELEX:32016R0679

REGULATION OF THE EUROPEAN PARLIAMENT AND OF THE COUNCIL LAYING DOWN HARMONISED RULES ON ARTIFICIAL INTELLIGENCE (ARTIFICIAL INTELLIGENCE ACT) AND AMENDING CERTAIN UNION LEGISLATIVE ACTS, 64 (2021). https://eur-lex.europa.eu/legal-content/EN/TXT/HTML/?uri=CELEX:52021PC0206

REGULATION (EU) 2022/2065 OF THE EUROPEAN PARLIAMENT AND OF THE COUNCIL of 19 October 2022 on a Single Market For Digital Services and amending Directive 2000/31/EC (Digital Services Act) (2022). https://eur-lex.europa.eu/eli/reg/2022/2065/oj/eng

Regulation (EU) 2024/1689, EU Artificial Intelligence Act, 144 (2024). https://artificialintelligenceact.eu/ai-act-explorer/

Executive Office of the President of the United States: Winning the Race. America's AI Action Plan. The White House (2025). www.whitehouse.gov

Gabriel, I.: Toward a theory of justice for artificial intelligence. Daedalus **151**(2), 218–231 (2022). https://research.ebsco.com/linkprocessor/plink?id=89621257-74bc-30b9-ba85-410993720997

Goode, L.: Life, but not as we know it: A.I. and the popular imagination. Cult. Unbound J. Current Cult. Res. **10**(2), 185–207 (2018). https://doi.org/10.3384/cu.2000.1525.2018102185

Gutting, G.: Foucault: A Very Short Introduction, vol. 122. Oxford University Press (2005)

Habermas, J.: Legitimation Crisis, vol. 519. Beacon Press (1975)

Hao, K.: This is how AI bias really happens—and why it's so hard to fix. MIT Technol. Rev. (2019)

Hintz, A., Dencik, L., Wahl-Jorgensen, K.: Digital Citizenship in a Datafied Society. Polity Press (2018)

Jones, M.L., Kaufman, E., Edenberg, E.: AI and the ethics of automating consent. IEEE Secur. Priv. Secur. Priv. **16**(3), 64–72 (2018). https://doi.org/10.1109/MSP.2018.2701155

Kaye, D.: Speech police: the global struggle to govern the Internet / David Kaye. Columbia Global Reports (2019). https://research.ebsco.com/linkprocessor/plink?id=584e56b7-59ec-3830-9f3d-aaafb26d5881

König, P.D., Wenzelburger, G.: Opportunity for renewal or disruptive force? How artificial intelligence alters democratic politics. Gov. Inf. Q. **37**(3), 101489 (2020). https://doi.org/10.1016/j.giq.2020.101489

Marino, M., Iacono, R., Mollerstrom, J.: (Mis-)Perceptions, information, and political polarization: a survey and a systematic literature review. Eur. J. Polit. Econ., 102578 (2024). https://doi.org/10.1016/j.ejpoleco.2024.102578

McCrory, L.: A feminist framework for urban AI governance: addressing challenges for public–private partnerships. Data Policy **6**, e79 (2024). https://doi.org/10.1017/dap.2024.69. Article e79

Molnar, P.: New technologies in migration: human rights impacts. Forced Migr. Rev. (61), 7–9 (2019). https://proxy.mau.se/login?url=https://search.ebscohost.com/login.aspx?direct=true&AuthType=ip,shib,cookie,url&db=asx&AN=137734618&site=eds-live&scope=site

Ram, J.: Moral decision-making in AI: a comprehensive review and recommendations. Technol. Forecast. Soc. Change **217**, 124150 (2025). https://doi.org/10.1016/j.techfore.2025.124150

Samarin, N., et al.: The medium is the message: how secure messaging apps leak sensitive data to push notification services (2024)

Sampath, P.G.: Governing artificial intelligence in an age of inequality. Global Pol. **12**, 21–31 (2021). https://doi.org/10.1111/1758-5899.12940

Strange, M.: Three different types of AI hype in healthcare. AI Ethics **4**, 1–8 (2024). https://doi.org/10.1007/s43681-024-00465-y

Teo, S.A.: How to think about freedom of thought (and opinion) in the age of AI. Comput. Law Secur. Rev. **53**, 105969 (2024). https://doi.org/10.1016/j.clsr.2024.105969

Tilmes, N.: Disability, fairness, and algorithmic bias in AI recruitment. Ethics Inf. Technol. **24**(2), 1–13 (2022). https://link-springer-com.proxy.mau.se/content/pdf/10.1007/s10676-022-09633-2.pdf

Vaara, E., Whittle, A.: Common sense, new sense or non-sense? a critical discursive perspective on power in collective sensemaking. J. Manage. Stud. **59**(3), 755–781 (2022). https://onlinelibrary.wiley.com/doi/full/10.1111/joms.12783

Vikhrov, I., Abdurakhimov, Z., Ashirbaev, S.: The use of big data in healthcare: lessons for developing countries from Uzbekistan. ZASTOSOWANIE BIG DATA W OCHRONIE ZDROWIA: INFORMACJE DLA KRAJÓW ROZWIJAJĄCYCH SIĘ NA PRZYKŁADZIE UZBEKISTANU **15**(2), 142–151 (2021). https://doi.org/10.5114/hpc.2021.106173

Zuboff, S.: Big other: surveillance capitalism and the prospects of an information civilization. J. Inf. Technol. **30**(1), 75–89 (2015). https://doi.org/10.1057/jit.2015.5

Zuboff, S.: Surveillance capitalism or democracy? The death match of institutional orders and the politics of knowledge in our information civilization. Organ. Theory **3**(3), 26317877221129290 (2022). https://doi.org/10.1177/26317877221129290

Zürn, M.: A theory of Global Governance: Authority, Legitimacy, and Contestation. Oxford University Press (2018)

Author Index

K. Nasrollahi et al. (Eds.): REPAI-W 2025, LNCS 16390, p. 119, 2026.
https://doi.org/10.1007/978-3-032-16886-3

MIX
Papier aus verantwortungsvollen Quellen
Paper from responsible sources
FSC® C105338

If you have any concerns about our products,
you can contact us on
ProductSafety@springernature.com

In case Publisher is established outside the EU,
the EU authorized representative is:
Springer Nature Customer Service Center GmbH
Europaplatz 3, 69115 Heidelberg, Germany

Printed by Libri Plureos GmbH
in Hamburg, Germany